The Targum Onqelos to Deuteronomy

The Aramaic Bible

• THE TARGUMS •

PROJECT DIRECTOR
Martin McNamara, M.S.C.

EDITORS
Kevin Cathcart • Michael Maher, M.S.C.
Martin McNamara, M.S.C.

EDITORIAL CONSULTANTS
Daniel J. Harrington, S.J. • Bernard Grossfeld
Alejandro Díez Macho, M.S.C.†

The Aramaic Bible

Volume 9

The Targum Onqelos to Deuteronomy

Translated, with Apparatus, and Notes

BY

Bernard Grossfeld

Michael Glazier, Inc.
Wilmington, Delaware

About the Translator:

Bernard Grossfeld is Professor of Hebrew and Aramaic at the University of Wisconsin-Milwaukee, and founding member of the Association for Targumic Studies. He holds a B.A. in Hebrew Literature from UCLA, an M.A. in Semitic Literature from the University of California-Berkeley, and a Ph.D. in Near Eastern Studies from Johns Hopkins University. Professor Grossfeld has published extensively on the Targum. He is the author of *A Bibliography of Targum Literature* (1972, 1977), *The First Targum of Esther* (1983) and its companion volume *Concordance of the First Targum to the Book of Esther* (1984), as well as the co-author of *Targum Onqelos on Genesis 49* (1976) and *Targum Onkelos to the Book of Genesis* (1982).

First published in 1988 by Michael Glazier, Inc., 1935 West Fourth Street, Wilmington, Delaware 19805.

Library of Congress Catalog Card Number: 86-45349
International Standard Book Number:
The Aramaic Bible Series: 0-89453-475-0
Targum Onqelos to Deuteronomy: 0-89453-488-2

Typography by Laura Burke
Logo design by Florence Bern.
Printed in the United States of America.

Table of Contents

Editors' Foreword

While any translation of the Scriptures may in Hebrew be called a Targum, the word is used especially for a translation of a book of the Hebrew Bible into Aramaic. Before the Christian era Aramaic had in good part replaced Hebrew in Palestine as the vernacular of the Jews. It continued as their vernacular for centuries later and remained in part as the language of the schools after Aramaic itself had been replaced as the vernacular.

Rabbinic Judaism has transmitted Targums of all books of the Hebrew Canon, with the exception of Daniel and Ezra-Nehemiah, which are themselves partly in Aramaic. We also have a translation of the Samaritan Pentateuch into the dialect of Samaritan Aramaic. From the Qumran Library we have sections of a Targum of Job and fragments of a Targum of Leviticus, chapter 16, facts which indicate that the Bible was being translated in Aramaic in pre-Christian times.

Translations of books of the Hebrew Bible into Aramaic for liturgical purposes must have begun before the Christian era, even though none of the Targums transmitted to us by Rabbinic Judaism can be shown to be that old and though some of them are demonstrably compositions from later centuries.

In recent decades there has been increasing interest among scholars and a larger public in these Targums. A noticeable lacuna, however, has been the absence of a modern English translation of this body of writing. It is in marked contrast with most other bodies of Jewish literature for which there are good modern English translations, for instance the Apocrypha and Pseudepigrapha of the Old Testament, Josephus, Philo, the Mishnah, the Babylonian Talmud and Midrashic literature, and more recently the Tosefta and Palestinian Talmud.

It is hoped that this present series will provide some remedy for this state of affairs.

The aim of the series is to translate all the traditionally-known Targums, that is those transmitted by Rabbinic Judaism, into modern English idiom, while at the same time respecting the particular and peculiar nature of what these Aramaic translations were originally intended to be. A translator's task is never an easy one. It is rendered doubly difficult when the text to be rendered is itself a translation which is at times governed by an entire set of principles.

All the translations in this series have been specially commissioned. The translators have made use of what they reckon as the best printed editions of the Aramaic Targum in question or have themselves directly consulted the manuscripts.

The translation aims at giving a faithful rendering of the Aramaic. The introduction to each Targum contains the necessary background information on the particular work. In general, each Targum translation is accompanied by an apparatus and notes. The former is concerned mainly with such items as the variant readings in the Aramaic texts, the relation of the English translation to the original, etc. The notes give what explanations the translator thinks necessary or useful for this series.

Not all the Targums here translated are of the same kind. Targums were translated at different times, and most probably for varying purposes, and have more than one interpretative approach to the Hebrew Bible. This diversity between the Targums themselves is reflected in the translation and in the manner in which the accompanying explanatory material is presented. However, a basic unity of presentation has been maintained. Targumic deviations from the Hebrew text, whether by interpretation or paraphrase, are indicated by italics.

A point that needs to be stressed with regard to this translation of the Targums is that by reason of the state of current targumic research, to a certain extent it must be regarded as a provisional one. Despite the progress made, especially in recent decades, much work still remains to be done in the field of targumic study. Not all the Targums are as yet available in critical editions. And with regard to those that have been critically edited from known manuscripts, in the case of the Targums of some books the variants between the manuscripts themselves are such as to give rise to the question whether they have all descended from a single common original.

Details regarding these points will be found in the various introductions and critical notes.

It is recognised that a series such as this will have a broad readership. The Targums constitute a valuable source of information for students of Jewish literature, particularly those concerned with the history of interpretation, and also for students of the New Testament, especially for those interested in its relationship to its Jewish origins. The Targums also concern members of the general public who have an interest in the Jewish interpretation of the Scriptures or in the Jewish background to the New Testament. For them the Targums should be both interesting and enlightening.

By their translations, introductions and critical notes the contributors to this series have rendered an immense service to the progress of targumic studies. It is hoped that the series, provisional though it may be, will bring significantly nearer the day when the definitive translation of the Targums can be made.

Kevin Cathcart   Martin McNamara, M.S.C.   Michael Maher, M.S.C.

PREFACE

The invitation by Father Martin McNamara to be responsible in this series for Targum Onqelos to the Torah was especially welcomed as it provided me, first of all in the Genesis volume, the chance to revise, expand, and update my earlier works *Targum Onqelos on Genesis 49,* Society of Biblical Literature Aramaic Studies 1, Missoula-Montana (Scholars Press), 1976, and *Targum Onkelos to Genesis,* New York (Ktav Publishing House, Inc.), 1982, both of which were co-authored with Professor Moses Aberbach, to whom I am grateful for his permission to utilize some of the ideas of our previous joint efforts. The present work by no means relegates the earlier ones to obscurity. The accompanying Aramaic text, as well as the existence of relevant passages, clauses, phrases, and even single words all in Hebrew characters, lend much value to the latter, while the detailed discussions in the former attest to its independent worth. Second, and far more significant to me, was this opportunity to present a study of Targum Onqelos to the entire Pentateuch. So far, no study exists in English on this official Targum treating its *modus operandum,* taking into consideration the vast relevant Rabbinic literature, comparing the Onqelos reading with that of the Septuagint, Vulgate, Peshitta, the Samaritan Hebrew and Aramaic Bibles, and other ancient versions, not to mention the other extant Targumim. Furthermore, the older standard commentaries in Hebrew have not yet been fully acknowledged by the scholarly world. They include not merely S.D. Luzzatto's classic *Oheb Ger,* and N. Adler's *Netina La-Ger,* works which are familiar to a limited audience of scholars, but also the Yemenite scholar Y. Korach's commentary on Targum Onqelos *Marpe Lashon,* a work rich in interpretive insight. This is of particular relevance in view of the well-known association of the Yemenite tradition with Targum Onqelos.

All of the above features have been incorporated into the Notes throughout the five books of the Pentateuch, together with any relevant finds from Qumran, or other recent discoveries of the Ancient Near East.

First and foremost, I would like to thank Father Martin McNamara, the project director, and Mr. Michael Glazier, the publisher, for inviting me to participate in this enterprise.

I am also grateful to the Wisconsin Society For Jewish Learning for their continual support of my research.

I thank Professor M. Goshen-Gottstein and the Institute For Advanced Studies of the Hebrew University in Jerusalem for providing me with a Research Fellowship during 1985-6, which gave me the opportunity to interact with scholars in this discipline with whom I formed part of the Targum and Aramaic Studies Group in residence there.

The very laborious task of inputting this manuscript into the computer, as well as the tedious work of checking the cross-references was done by Clare Pfann of Jerusalem, who rose to the challenge at hand with results of the highest quality.

Due credit must also go to my research assistants Sharon Slavin and Christine Gilbert for their meticulous proofreading of the galleys, as well as the preparation of the index.

Last but not least, I gratefully acknowledge the assistance of my wife Sylvia, in proofreading the early computer version of the manuscript, as well as for the patience and encouragement she has given me these past years.

Bernard Grossfeld
Milwaukee, Wisconsin

ABBREVIATIONS

Abot R. Nat	*Aboth de Rabbi Nathan,* ed. S. Schechter. Vienna, 1887.
Afo	Archiv für Orientforschung.
Agg. Ber.	*Aggadath Bereshith,* ed. S. Buber. Krakow, 1903.
ALUOS	Annual of the Leeds University Oriental Society. Leiden.
Ant.	*Antiquities of the Jews*—Josephus. The Loeb Classical Library, ed.
Ber. Rab.	*Midrash Bereshith Rabbati,* ed. C. Albeck. Jerusalem, 1940.
BHM	*Beth Ha-Midrash,* ed. A. Jellinek. Second edition. Jerusalem, 1938.
Biblica	Biblica. Rome.
Cant. Rab.	Canticles Rabbah in *Midrash Rabba al Ḥamishah Ḥumshe Torah veḤamesh Megillot.* Vilna, 1884-7.
CTgA,B,C,D,E,F	*Masoreten Des Westens* by Paul Kahle. Stuttgart, 1930.
Deut. Rab.	*Deuteronomy Rabba,* ed. S. Lieberman. Jerusalem, 1940 (if page numbers are given) also in *Midrash Rabba al Ḥamisha Ḥumshe Torah veḤamesh Megillot.* Vilna, 1884-7.
Ekh. Rab.	Ekha Rabbati, ed. S. Buber. Vilna, 1899.
Esth. Rab.	Esther Rabba in *Midrash Rabba al Ḥamishah Ḥumshe Torah veḤamesh Megillot.* Vilna, 1884-7.
Exod. Rab.	Exodus Rabbah in *Midrash Rabba al Ḥamishah Ḥumshe Torah veḤamesh Megillot.* Vilna, 1884-7.
Frg. Tg.	*The Fragment-Targums to the Pentateuch,* ed. M. Klein. Rome, 1980.
Gen. Rab.	Genesis Rabba acc. to *Bereshith Rabba,* ed. J. Theodor. Jerusalem, 1965.

Hakarmel	Hakarmel. Vilna, 1860-70 (Hebrew Periodical).
HTR	Harvard Theological Review. Cambridge, Mass.
HUCA	Hebrew Union College Annual. Cincinnati.
ICC	International Critical Commentary. Edinburgh, 1901-
IEJ	Israel Exploration Journal. Jerusalem.
JB Jud GL	Jahrbücher für jüdische Geschichte und Literatur. Frankfurt a.M., 1874-92.
JBL	Journal of Biblical Literature.
JHS	Journal of Hebrew Studies. New York, 1969.
JJS	Journal of Jewish Studies. London.
JQR	Jewish Quarterly Review. Philadelphia.
JSOT	Journal for the Study of the Old Testament.
JTS	Journal of Theological Studies. Oxford, London.
Kokhebe Yishaq	Kokhebe Yiṣḥaq. Vienna 1845-1869, 1873 (Hebrew Periodical).
Leq. Tob	*Midrash Leqaḥ Tob,* ed. S. Buber. Lvov, 1878.
Lev. Rab.	Leviticus Rabba acc. to *Wayyiqra Rabba,* ed. M. Margulies. Jerusalem, 1953-60.
Magazin	Magazin für judische Geschichte und Literature. Berlin, 1874-5.
Mek	*Mechilta D'Rabbi Ismael,* ed. H.S. Horovitz and I.A. Rabin. Jerusalem, 1970.
MGWJ	Monatsschrift für Geschishte und Wissenschaft des Judentums.
MHG	*Midrash Haggadol* on Genesis, ed. M. Margulies. Jerusalem, 1946-7; on Exodus, ed. M. Margulies. Jerusalem, 1956.
Mid. Agg.	*Midrash Aggadah,* ed. S. Buber. Vienna, 1893-4.
MRSBY	*Mekhilta de Rabbi Shimon ben Yoḥai,* ed. J.N. Epstein. Jerusalem, 1955.
Num.Rab.	Numbers Rabba in *Midrash Rabba al Ḥamisha Ḥumshe Torah veḤamesh Megillot.* Vilna, 1884-7.
PR	*Pesiqta Rabbati,* ed. M. Friedmann. Vilna, 1880.
PRE	Pirqe Rabbi Eliezer. Jerusalem, 1973 (based on 1544 Venice edition).

PRK	*Pesiqta de Rab Kahana,* ed. S. Buber. Lyck, 1868.
Sam. Tg.	*The Samaritan Targum of the Pentateuch,* ed. A. Tal. Tel-Aviv, 1980-1.
SBL	Society of Biblical Literature.
Sekh. Tob	*Midrash Sekhel Tob,* ed. S. Buber. Lvov, 1900.
Shoh. Tob	*Midrash Shoḥer Tob,* ed. S. Buber. Vilna, 1862.
Sifra	*Sifra debe Rab,* ed. I.H. Weiss. Vienna, 1862.
Sifre (Numbers)	*Siphre D'Be Rab,* ed. H.S. Horovitz. Jerusalem, 1966.
Sifre	*Siphre on Deuteronomy,* ed. L. Finkelstein. New York, 1969.
ST	Studia Theologica. Oslo.
Syr.	*The Syriac Bible.* United Bible Societies, 1979.
Tanh(A)	*Midrash Tanḥuma.* Warsaw, 1875.
Tanh(B)	*Midrash Tanḥuma,* ed. S. Buber. Vilna, 1885.
Tarbiz	Tarbiz. Jerusalem (Hebrew Periodical).
Textus	Textus. Annual of the Hebrew University Bible Project. Jerusalem.
Tg. Neof.	*Neophyti I,* ed. A. Díez Macho. Madrid, 1968-78.
Tg. Onq.	*The Bible in Aramaic: The Pentateuch acc. to Targum Onkelos,* ed. A. Sperber. Leiden, 1959.
Tg. Ps.-Jon.	*Targum Jonathan ben Uzziel,* ed. D. Rieder. Jerusalem, 1984-5.
Tg.Ket.	*The Bible in Aramaic: The Hagiographa,* ed. A. Sperber. Leiden, 1968.
Tg.Neb.	*The Bible in Aramaic: The Former Prophets acc. to Targum Jonathan,* ed. A Sperber. Leiden, 1959; *The Latter Prophets acc. Targum Jonathan,* ed. A Sperber. Leiden, 1962.
VT	Vetus Testamentum. Leiden.
VT Sup	Vetus Testamentum Supplement. Leiden.
Yalq. Makh.	*Yalqut Ha-Makhiri,* ed. S. Buber. Berdichev, 1900.
Yalq. Shim.	*Yalqut Shimoni:Sepher Bereshith,* ed. D. Heimann et al. Jerusalem, 1973; *Sepher Shemoth,* ed. D. Heimann et al. Jerusalem, 1977, 1980.
ZAW	Zeitschrift für die alttestamentlische Wissenschaft. Berlin.

Transcription

Consonant			*Vowel*	
'	א		e	◌ֶ
b	בּ		ē	◌ֵ
ḇ	ב		ê	◌ֵי
g	ג		ī	◌ִ
d	ד		î	◌ִי
h	ה		a	◌ַ
w	ו		ā	◌ָ
z	ז		o	◌ָ
ḥ	ח		ŏ	◌ֳ
ṭ	ט		ă	◌ֲ
y	י		ĕ	◌ֱ
k	כּ		ě	◌ְ
ḵ	כ,	ך	ū	◌ֻ
l	ל		û	וּ
m	מ,	ם	ō	◌ֹ
n	נ,	ן	ô	וֹ
s	ס			
ʿ	ע			
p	פּ			
p̄	פ,	ף		
ṣ	צ,	ץ		
q	ק			
r	ר			
š	שׁ			
ś	שׂ			
t	תּ			
ṯ	ת			

Note

A critical Introduction to all books of Targum Onqelos can be found in *The Targum Onqelos to Genesis,* Volume 6 of this series.

Translation

CHAPTER 1

1. These are the words that Moses spoke *with*[1] the Israelites on the other side of the Jordan; *he rebuked them for having sinned*[2] in the wilderness *and for having caused provocation*[2] in the plains opposite the *Sea of Reeds*[2]; at Paran *they talked irreverently about the Manna*[2]; and at Ḥaṣeroth *they caused provocation about the meat*[2]*; and because they had made the golden calf.*[2] 2. It is a *march*[3] of eleven days from Horeb by way of Mount Seir until *Reqem Geah.*[4] 3. Now in the fortieth year, in the eleventh month, on the first {day} of the month, Moses spoke to the Israelites in accordance to all {the instructions} that the Lord had commanded him for them, 4. after he had defeated Sihon, the Amorite king, who dwelt at Ḥeshbon, and Og king of *Maṯnan,*[5] who dwelt at Ashtaroth in Edrei. 5. On the other side of the Jordan in the land of Moab did Moses begin to expound *the teaching of*[6] this Law, as follows: 6. "The Lord our God spoke to us at Horeb, saying, 'You have stayed long enough at this mountain. 7. Turn and set out in the direction of the hill country of the Amorite and all its neighboring areas, in the Arabah, in the lowlands, in the south, and in the seacoast, the land of the Canaanites, and to Lebanon as far as the Great River, the river Euphrates. 8. Realize, I have placed this land before you; go up and take possession of this land which I promised by oath to your ancestors—(to) Abraham, (to) Isaac, and (to) Jacob, to give to them and to their descendants after them.' 9. Then I said to you at that time as follows: 'I am not able to bear {the burden of} you by myself. 10. The Lord your God has increased you so you are

Notes, Chapter 1

[1]See Lev. Chap. 1, n. 1.

[2]The Hebrew is vague and concise—it begins with "These are the words that Moses spoke to all of Israel on the other side of the Jordan" and then continues with the *non sequitur* "through the wilderness, in the Arabah near Suph, between Paran and Tophel, Laban, Ḥaṣeroth, and Di-Zahab." The Targum connects these two passages by inserting "he rebuked them for," and then inserts "for" at the beginning of each clause, which deals with an incident that displayed Israel's ungratefulness towards God at each of the place-names mentioned in the Hebrew. The phrase "he rebuked them," although only stated once, is meant for all subsequent clauses. These expansions, some of which are explanations of the place-names, are widespread throughout Rabbinic literature and hereby follow in order:

I. "he rebuked them" *PRK* XIII *Diḇrê Yirmiyāhû* (p. 112a) "R. Tanḥuma in the name of R. Eleazar ... in Scripture, whenever a word or words from the root *dbr* as *dāḇār, diḇrê, dĕḇārîm* occurs, curses and *rebuke* are to follow."

Ibid. Wĕzō't Habĕrāḵāh XXXI (p. 197a) "Inasmuch as at the beginning of Deuteronomy, Moses *rebukes* Israel—'These are the words which Moses spoke to all of Israel' (Deut. 1:1)." Cf. also Exod. Rab. LI:8; Eccl. Rab. III:11; and Sifre Debarim I (ed. Finkelstein, p. 4).

II. "*for having sinned* in the wilderness" (Hebrew—"in the wilderness")

1. *Midrash Debarim Rabbah* VIII (p. 5): "Rather he rebuked them on the other side of the Jordan for what they did in the wilderness, as it says 'how often they rebelled against Him in the wilderness' (Ps. 78:40)."

2. *Sifre* (*ibid.*) "'In the wilderness' (Deut 1:11)—this teaches (us) that he rebuked them for what they did in the wilderness."

today as numerous as the stars of heaven. 11. May the Lord, God of your ancestors, increase you a thousand times, and bless you as He has *promised*[7] you. 12. How can I alone bear your problems, and your affairs, as well as your disputes. 13. Provide for yourselves men who are wise, (and) discerning and knowledgeable among your tribes, and I will appoint them as chiefs over you.' 14. Then you replied to me and said, 'What you *proposed*[8] to do is good.' 15. So I took the chiefs of your tribes, men who were wise

Notes, Chapter 1 (Cont.)

III. "*for having caused provocation* in the plains" (Hebrew *bā'ărāḇāh*)

1. *Debarim Rabbah* (*ibid.*) *bā'ărāḇāh* for what they did at Shittim."

2. *Sifre* (*ibid.*) "'In the Arabah' (Deut. 1:1), this teaches (us) that he rebuked them for what they did in the Plains of Moab, as it says 'and Israel dwelled at Shittim. . .' (Num. 25:1)."

IV. "Sea of Reeds" (Hebrew *sûp̱*)

1. *Sifre* (*ibid.*) "'Opposite *sûp̱*' (Deut. 1:1)—this teaches (us) that he rebuked them for what they did at the Sea (of Reeds), in that they rebelled at the Sea (of Reeds)."

2. *'Abot R. Nat.* XXXIV (Vers. A, p. 98). "'opposite *sûp̱*' (Deut. 1:1)—for having rebelled at the Sea of Reeds. R. Judah said: They rebelled at the Sea (and) they rebelled in the Sea, as it says, 'They rebelled at the Sea, in the Sea of Reeds' (Ps. 106:7)."

V. "at Paran they talked irreverently about the Manna." (Hebrew "between Paran and [between] Tophel and Laban").

1. *Debarim Rabbah* (*ibid.*, p. 6) "R. Simeon b. Yoḥai said: I reviewed the 42 travel stations and found no place by the name of Tophel. Then what does Tophel mean? Words of irreverence which they brought forth against the Manna whose name is Laban ('white'), as it says, 'now the Manna was like coriander seed' (Num. 11:7)."

2. *Sifre* (*ibid.*, p. 5) "'and between Tophel and Laban' (Deut. 1:1)—words of irreverence by which they spoke degradingly of the Manna, and so it says: 'and our soul loathes this miserable food' (Num. 21:5)."

3. *'Abot R. Nat.* (*ibid.*, p. 99) "'and between Tophel' (Deut. 1:1)—these were the irreverent words which they uttered over the Manna."

VI. "and at Ḥaṣeroth *they caused provocation about the meat*" (Hebrew "and *Ḥaṣeroth*").

1. *'Abot R. Nat.* (*ibid.*) "'And Ḥaṣeroth' (Deut. 1:1) refers to the incident of the quail" (cf. Num. 11:35 and Tg. Ps.-Jon. thereon).

VII. "*and because they had made the golden calf*" [*Hebrew "and Di-Zahab"*).

1. *Sifre* (*ibid.*, p. 6) "'And Di-Zahab' (Deut. 1:1)—he said to them this outdid everything else that you did. The deed of the golden calf is more hard on me than everything else."

2. *b. Ber.* 32a "What is 'and Di-Zahab' (Deut. 1:1)? They said in the school of R. Jannai: Thus spoke Moses before the Holy One, blessed be He: Sovereign of the Universe, the silver and the gold (*zahab*) which You showered upon Israel until they said: Enough (*dai*), that it was which led to their making the calf."

3. *Debarim Rabbah* (*ibid.*) "'and Di-Zahab' (Deut. 1:1)—R. Pinkhas in the name of R. Abbahu said: Moses came to rebuke them for the deed of the calf, said the Holy One, blessed be He: Enough (*dai*). . ."

4. *'Abot R. Nat.* (*ibid.*) "'and Di-Zahab' (Deut. 1:1)—said Aaron to them: Enough (*dai*) for you is the sin of the gold (*zahab*) which you brought for the calf."

[3]An insertion implied in the concise Hebrew text. The Syr. has *mrd'*—"march," Tg. Ps.-Jon. has *mhlk*, the identical term of Tg. Onq. as does the Frg. Tg. (P, V), while Tg. Neof. has *'rḥ mhlk* "the distance of a march," while Tg. Neof. m. has *'rḥ* "distance," only.

[4]See Num. Chap. 32, n. 6.

[5]See Num. Chap. 21, n. 23.

[6]An insertion, implied in the Hebrew. This term—*ulpan*—occurs in the Targum to Gen. 49:11, and there too is associated with the Law—(Torah). Tg. Ps.-Jon. likewise employs this root, but in the form of the verb *'lp* in the infinitive as a translation for the Hebrew "expound" in this verse.

[7]Lit. "spoken to."

[8]Lit. "have spoken."

and knowledgeable, and I appointed them chiefs over you: chiefs over thousands, and chiefs over hundreds, as well as chiefs over fifties and chiefs over tens, and officers over your tribes. 16. Moreover, I commanded your judges at that time, saying, 'Hear <the disputes> between your brothers and judge honestly between man and his fellowman and (between) *the*[a] stranger. 17. Do not show partiality in judgment; you should *hear*[b] small and great alike; do not be afraid of anyone, for judgment belongs to the Lord; and the matter that is too difficult for you, you should bring to me and I shall hear it.' 18. Then I commanded you at that time the various things you should do. 19. So we set out from Horeb, and went through that great and terrible wilderness which you saw along the road to the hill country of the Amorite, as the Lord our God commanded us, and so we came to *Reqem Geah,*[4] 20. Then I said to you: 'You have come to the hill country of the Amorite that the Lord our God is giving us. 21. Realize that the Lord your God has placed *this*[9] land before you; proceed to take possession <of it> as the Lord, the God of your ancestors has promised you; do not be afraid nor be discouraged.' 22. Then all of you approached me and said, 'Let us send out men ahead of us that they may spy out the land for us, then bring us back a report on the road we should *take,*[10] and the cities we should enter.' 23. The idea was pleasing to me, so I *selected*[11] twelve men, one man from each tribe. 24. So you turned (and), went up into the hill country, and arrived at the Valley of the Cluster which you spied out. 25. Then they brought down to us some of the fruit of the land which they had taken themselves and brought us back word saying, 'It is a good land that the Lord our God is giving to us.' 26. But you did not want to go up and rebelled against the *Memra*[12] of the Lord your God. 27. Moreover, you grumbled in your tents saying, 'Because the Lord hates us, has He brought us out of the land of Egypt, so as to deliver us into the hands of the Amorite to destroy us? 28. Whereto are we going? Our brethren have *discouraged us*[13] saying: A people more numerous and more *powerful*[14] than us, large cities fortified up to the heavens, as well as the descendants of the *giant*[c] have we seen there.' 29. So I said to you, 'Do not be discouraged, and do not fear them. 30. The Lord your God who marches ahead of you, *His Memra*[15] will *fight*[d] for you, just as He did everything for you in Egypt before your <very> eyes, 31. and in the wilderness where you saw how the Lord your God carried you as a man carries his son, all the way that you travelled until you came to this place. 32. Yet in spite of this thing you did not trust *the Memra of*[15] the Lord your God, 33. Who marches ahead of you on the way to prepare for you a site for a resting place, to allow you to encamp, with a pillar of fire by night and a pillar of cloud by day to show you the road on which you should travel.' 34. Then *the sound of*[e] your words *were heard before the Lord*[16] and He became angry and swore as follows: 35. 'Not a single one of these men, this evil generation, shall see the good land that I swore to give to *your*[f] ancestors. 36. Except for Caleb son of Jephunneh; he will see it and to him I will give the land upon which he treads as well as to his descendants in exchange for

Apparatus, Chapter 1

[a] V, G, and v have: "his," as does the Hebrew.
[b] d_2 and l have: "receive."
[c] J, G, and V have the plural, so does the Hebrew.
[d] D and h add: "the war."
[e] c has: "all," reading *kl* in place of *ql*.
[f] So also B, M, j, v, b, and c, as well as the Hebrew, whereas Sperber's main text has: "their," as do the Syr. and some LXX mss. (for which cf. BH Stuttgartensia).
[g] A adds: "against him."
[h] D adds: "resting."

having *completely followed the reverence of the Lord.*[17] 37. Also against me *was there anger from before the Lord*[18] on account of you, saying, 'You shall not enter there, either. 38. Joshua, son of Nun who attends you, he will enter there, him you should encourage, for he will give it as a possession to Israel. 39. Moreover, your little ones who you said would be plundered, and your children who do not yet know this day good from bad, they will enter there, for to them will I give it and they {are the ones who} will inherit it. 40. As for you, turn and set out for the wilderness along the route to the Sea of Reeds.' 41. Then you replied saying to me, 'We have sinned *before*[19] the Lord; we shall go up and wage war according to everything that the Lord has commanded us, and each one of you girded himself with his war gear *and we began*[20] to go up to the hill country.' 42. Whereupon the Lord said to me, 'Tell them they should not go up nor should they wage *war,*[g] for *My Shekhina*[21] is *not*[h] among you, so that you should not become *shattered*[22] before your enemies.' 43. So I spoke with you; however, you did not listen but rebelled against the *Memra*[12] of the Lord and presumptuously went up to the hill country. 44. Then the Amorite, who dwelt in that hill country, went out against you and pursued you as bees *spring forth,*[23] *and beat them into a retreat*[24] from Seir as far as

Notes, Chapter 1 (Cont.)

[9]Lit. "the."
[10]Lit. "go up."
[11]Lit. "took."
[12]See Exod. Chap. 17, n. 1.
[13]Lit. "melted our hearts."
[14]See Num. Chap. 24, n. 14.
[15]See Introduction VII D. 1.
[16]See Gen. Chap. 29, n. 9.
[17]See Num. Chap. 14, n. 24.
[18]The Hebrew has: "was the Lord angry," which is an anthropomorphism and accordingly circumvented by being transformed into the passive involving the noun anger and the particle *qdm.*
[19]See Gen. Chap. 4, n. 1.
[20]The Targum renders the enigmatic Hebrew *wattāhînû* interpretively to mean "and we began" from the Aramaic *šry.* Tg. Ps.-Jon. is identical here, whereas Tg. Neof. has "and hurried" (*yḥy*), and the Syr. "got excited" (*grg*).
[21]See Introduction VII D.3.
[22]See Lev. Chap. 26, n. 16.
[23]The Hebrew has: "do," which is vague and here interpretively rendered by the specific action implied in "do," i.e., "spring forth." This translation in the Targum is cited *in toto* in the following Talmudic passage—b. Sot. 48b "R. Joshua b. Levi said: It is the honey which comes from the hills [*ṣoḇim*]. How is this known? *As R. Shesheth translated* (*Deut. 1:44—'as the bees do'*): *When the bees spring forth* and fly in the heights of the world and collect honey from the herbage on the mountains."
[24]The Hebrew has: "defeated" which is here interpretively translated to mean "beat them into a retreat" in view of what follows in the text "*from* Seir *as far as* Ḥormah." This fact alone was sufficient reason for the Targum not to translate Hebrew *nkh* here by the regular equivalents *mḥy* (here used by Ps.-Jon. and the Sam. Tg. [J] in the form of *m'y*), and *qṭl* (here employed by the Frg. Tg. [V]). Ps.-Jon., the Sam. Tg. (J), the Frg. Tg. (V), Tg. Neof. (which has *ktt*—"crush") all, however, render the following word Seir by *bgbwl*—"at Gabal," whereas the Syr. which has *ṭrd* here, the identical root of Tg. Onq., follows it by the preposition *mn* (as does the LXX *'από*, and Vg. *de*). This preposition necessitated the interpretive rendering "beat into a retreat" an action which is compatible with a prepositional clause starting with "*from* . . . unto" a sequence which follows here. In this respect the preposition *b* here in the Hebrew and in the Targum has been rendered "from" rather than "in" or "at." See, in fact, S.R. Driver's remarks in *Deuteronomy: A Critical and Exegetical Commentary* (*ICC*). New York (Charles Scribner's Sons), 1902, p. 31, where he proposes a *b/m*

Hormah. 45. So you returned and wept before the Lord, but the Lord did not *accept your prayer*[25] nor listened to *your words.*[26] 46. Thereafter you stayed at *Reqem*[27] many days, as long as you stayed <at all the other places>.

CHAPTER 2

1. Then we turned and set out for the wilderness along the route to the Sea of Reeds as the Lord had spoken to me, and we encompassed the hill country of Seir many days. 2 Then the Lord said to me as follows: 3. 'You have encompassed this hill country long enough, <now> turn north. 4. Now the people you should command as follows: You will be passing through the territory of your brethren, the descendants of Esau who dwell in Seir, and they will be afraid of you; still be very careful. 5 Do not provoke them, for I will not give you any of their land, not even enough to put your foot on, for I have given the hill country of Seir as an inheritance to Esau. 6. You may buy from them with money *grain*[1] for eating; also, you may buy from them with money water for drinking. 7. For the Lord your God has blessed you in all *your work;*[2] *He has supplied you your needs*[3] when you travelled through this great wilderness; these forty years *the Memra of the Lord your God*[a4] was *your support;*[b] you lacked nothing.' 8. Thereafter we went past our brethren, the descendants of Esau, who lived in Seir away from the route of the plains, away from Elath and from Ezion-Geber, and turned away, then passed on to the route along the Wilderness of Moab. 9. Then the Lord said to me, 'Do not oppress the Moabites nor *cause any provocation in order to engage them in battle,*[5] for I have not given you any of *their*[c] land as an inheritance, rather I have given *Leḥayath*[6] to the descendants of Lot as an inheritance. 10. Formerly the "fear inspiring ones" dwelt in it, a people great and numerous as well as *powerful*[7] as the giants. 11. The giants themselves considered them as giants, and it was the Moabites who called them *fear inspiring ones.* 12. Likewise, the Horites formerly lived at Seir, then the descendants of Esau dispossessed them and destroyed them from before them, then replaced them, as did Israel to the land they were to inherit, which the Lord had given them. 13. Now, proceed to cross the Wadi of Zered'; so we crossed the Wadi of Zered. 14. Moreover, the period that we traveled from *Reqem Geah*[8] until we crossed the Wadi of Zered came to thirty-eight years, until that entire generation of war-waging men had perished from the camp, just as the Lord had sworn concerning them. 15. Also a plague from before the Lord *emanated*[9] against them, to destroy them from the midst of the camp, until they ceased to exist. 16. Now when all the war-waging men had ceased to die from among the

Apparatus, Chapter 2

[a] (d_1 = y) d has: "the Lord your God, His Memra."
[b] D has: "with you."
[c] D, G, and v have: "his," as does the Hebrew.
[d] J, D, and b have: "to."
[e] i has: "inheriting."
[f] D has: "Peṣiaḥ," which may be a place-name, or even a literal translation of the Hebrew—"village."
[g] G has: "then."

people, 17. the Lord spoke *with*[d] me as follows: 18. 'Today you are passing through the territory of Moab, through *Leḥayath,*[6] 19. and will then approach *the area of*[10] the Ammonites; do not oppress them, nor provoke <them> *so as to wage war against them,*[11] for I will not give any part of the land of the Ammonite descendants to you as an inheritance, as I have given it to the descendants of Lot as an inheritance. 20. It too is considered as the territory of the giants; the giants lived there formerly, and the Ammonites called them schemers. 21. A nation, great, numerous and as *powerful*[7] as giants, but the Lord destroyed them in advance of them and they *dispossessed*[e] them and dwelt in their place. 22. Just as He did to the descendants of Esau who dwelt at Seir, who had destroyed the Horites from before them, by dispossessing them and dwelling in their place to this day. 23. As for the Avites who dwelt at *Rephiaḥ*[f] as far as Gaza, the Cappodocians, who came from Cappodocia, destroyed them and dwelt in their place. 24. Proceed to set out and cross the Wadi of Arnon; realize that I have delivered into your control Siḥon, the king of Ḥeshbon, the Amorite, and his territory; start to expel *him*[12] and cause a provocation so as to make war against *him.*[g] 25. This day I begin to

Notes, Chapter 1 (Cont.)

confusion in the Hebrew of this verse on the basis of palaeography. Cf. Num. 14:45 where the same situation holds true.

[25]See Gen. Chap. 16, n. 1 and 5.

[26]The Hebrew "you" is here interpretively rendered; so also Tgs. Neof. and Ps.-Jon.

[27]See Gen. Chap. 14, n. 8.

Notes, Chapter 2

[1]See Gen. Chap. 41, n. 14.

[2]Lit. "the work of your hands."

[3]The Hebrew has *yāda'* "has taken notice of," lit. "(God) knows," which due to the anthropomorphic factor is here paraphrased by the Targum to apply to the needs of the Israelites during their sojourning through the wilderness. A similar situation exists in 32:10 below, where the Hebrew "He found him in the wilderness territory" is paraphrased in the Targum "He supplied their needs in the wilderness territory," to avoid the notion of God "finding," and, especially, Hos. 13:5 "I knew you in the wilderness" = "I supplied your needs in the wilderness" (Tg. Neb.). Tg. Ps.-Jon. is here identical, whereas Tg. Neof. paraphrases "it is revealed before Me."

[4]See Gen. Chap. 26, n. 2.

[5]The Hebrew "provoke them to war" is concise, and accordingly expanded by the Targum who inserts "in order to engage."

[6]See Num. Chap. 21, n. 9.

[7]See Num. Chap. 24, n. 14.

[8]See Num. Chap. 32, n. 6.

[9]Lit. "was."

[10]Lit. "opposite."

[11]An insertion, no doubt influenced by vss. 9, 24 where it exists at this point in the Hebrew, though no such insertion occurs in vs. 5 above. Tgs. Ps.-Jon. and Neof. as well as the LXX similarly insert it in the present verse.

[12]An addition, to supply a direct object for the preceding imperative *rāš*. The Hebrew implies it, whereas the Vg. supplies it in the form of "the earth" (*et terram*) in line with its translation of the Hebrew imperative *rāš* as "possess," rather than "dispossess," or "expel," the same vein in which the LXX and Tg. Neof. understood the word, whereas Tg. Ps.-Jon. understood it as "dispossess" or "expel," and likewise adds the suffix of the third masc. sing. pronoun. The whole question of Hebrew *yrš* meaning "to inherit" or "dispossess" mainly depends on the conjugation. In the *qal* it essentially has the former; in the *hiphil* the latter. This is reflected in the Targum who renders the former by the Aramaic equivalent of *yrt,* and the latter

put the dread and fear of you upon the nations everywhere under the heavens, so that they will hear of your reputation and tremble and *become humbled*[h] towards you.' 26. Then I sent messengers from the Wilderness of Kedemoth to Siḥon, king of Ḥeshbon, with words of peace, saying, 27. 'Let me pass through your country; I will go only on the main road, and will not turn off to the right or to the left. 28. You may sell me *grain*[1] for money so that I could eat, and water you may give me for money so that I could drink, only let me pass through on foot. 29. Just as the descendants of Esau who dwell in Seir and the Moabites who dwell in *Leḥayath*[6] did for me, until I cross the Jordan into the land, which the Lord our God is giving us.' 30. But Siḥon, king of Ḥeshbon, did not want to let us pass through his territory, for the Lord your God had made his spirit stubborn and had made his heart obstinate, in order to deliver him into your control, as He has done now. 31. Then the Lord said to me, 'Realize that I have begun to deliver Siḥon and his land *to*[13] you; start to expel *him*[12] in order to take possession of his land.' 32. Thereupon Siḥon, he and his entire people, went out towards us to wage war at Jahaz. 33. But the Lord our God delivered him *to*[13] us, and we defeated him and his sons, as well as all his people. 34. Then we conquered all his cities at that time and put an end to all the cities, men, women, and children; we left no survivors. 35. Only the livestock we plundered for ourselves, as well as the spoil of the cities we had conquered. 36. From Aroer that is on the edge of the Arnon valley, as well as the city within the valley itself as far as Gilead, there was no city too mighty for us; all of them did the Lord our God deliver to us. 37. Except you did not encroach on the territory of the Ammonites, all along the edge of the Wadi of *Jubbeka*[i] and the cities of the hill country, and everywhere else the Lord our God had commanded.

Apparatus, Chapter 2 (Cont.)

[h] C and d_2 have: "be in anguish," as does the Hebrew.

[i] I has: "Jabbok."

Apparatus, Chapter 3

[a] The root *msr* is here interpretive, whereas i_a has the literal *yhb* "gave."

[b] D and g omit, as in Lev. 25:29 and 31.

[c] k has the plural.

[d] I has the interpretive: "conquered."

[e] j has the singular collective, as does the Hebrew.

Notes, Chapter 2 (Cont.)

by *trk* "dispossess" or "expel." However, there are instances when confusion sets in, and a variety of translations are reflected by different Targum manuscripts, with other Ancient Versions even entering the picture. For example Num. 14:24 when the Hebrew has *yôrišénnāh,* a clear *hiphil* form, yet the Targum (in Sperber's main text) renders *yyrtwnh* as if the Hebrew read *yîrāšénnāh,* a reading that in fact exists in the Sam. Heb. Yet, a number of Targum mss. (v, g, F, and Rashi's version of the Targum) have *ytrknh.* In the present chapter vss. 12, 21, 22 have *yîrāšûm* in the Hebrew, a clear *qal,* yet the Targum translates them *trykwnwn* "dispossess" in each case (only in vs. 21 is there a variant [i] which has *wyrytwnwn*). In Num. 32:39 the Hebrew *wayôreš* is a *hiphil;* the Targum has the expected *wtryk,* yet Sperber lists a variant(s) which reads *w'rytw* implying a Hebrew *Vorlage wyyrš* (*qal*).

[13]Lit. "before."

CHAPTER 3

1. Then we turned and went up along the road to *Maṯnan,*[1] and Og, king of *Maṯnan,*[1] he and his entire people went out towards us to Edrei to wage war. 2. Whereupon the Lord said to me, 'Do not be afraid of him, for I am delivering him and his entire people and his land into your control, and you will do to him just as you did to Siḥon, king of the Amorites, who dwelt at Ḥeshbon.' 3. So the Lord our God also *delivered*[a] into our control Og, king of *Maṯnan,*[1] and his entire people, and we defeated him leaving no survivors. 4. Then we conquered all his cities at that time; there was not a city which we did not take from him, sixty cities, the area of the province of *Trachonitis,*[2] the kingdom of Og in *Maṯnan.*[1] 5. All these cities were fortified with *high*[b] *wall,*[c] gates and bars, besides a large number of unwalled cities. 6. Then we put an end to them as we did to Siḥon, king of Ḥeshbon; we put an end to all the cities—men, women, and children. 7. While all of the livestock and spoil of the cities we plundered for ourselves. 8. At that time we *took*[d] the territory from the two Amorite kings on this side of the Jordan from the Wadi of Arnon as far as Mount Hermon, 9. the Sidonians called Hermon Sirion, while the *Amorites*[e] called it *Mountain of Snow,*[3] 10. all the cities of the

Notes, Chapter 3

[1]See Num. Chap. 21, n. 23.

[2]The Hebrew has Argob, which the Targum here renders by the area known as τραχωνίτιδοζ mentioned in the N.T. (Luke 3:1). According to D.C. Pellett (*Interpreter's Dictionary of the Bible* 4 [1962]: p. 676f.) the area is a portion of the N. Transjordan plateau which was known as Bashan in the O.T., and called Hauran in modern times. It was defined in general terms given by Josephus (*Ant.* XV: 10.3) as being 25 miles south of Damascus, along its SW border was Batanaea (= Bashan, *Ant.* XVII:2.1). Eusebius in his Onomastica Sacra mentions it (# 912, of E.Z. Melamed's *The Onomastikon of Eusebius.* Jerusalem [The Hebrew University] 1966, p. 81f.) and locates it on the other side of Boṣra in the desert, south, facing Damascus. In fact, the Jerusalem Talmud (y. Šeb. VI:1, p. 36c) also locates it as "bordering on Boṣra," as does t. *Šeb. IV:11 and Sifre Éqeb* LI, p. 118. The Greek word for Trachonitis is properly an adjective, though the name of the district is at times given as a noun, as here meaning "a rough, stony district." Cf. further S.R. Driver, *Deuteronomy* (*ICC*), op. cit., p. 48ff. on this identification.

[3]The Hebrew has: "Senir," which the Targum here renders "snow-mountain." In their annotated English translation of Rashi (*Pentateuch with Targum Onkelos, Haphtaroth and Rashi's Commentary: Deuteronomy.* New York [Hebrew Publishing Co.], 1934, p. 188f.), M. Rosenbaum and A.M. Silbermann comment on Rashi's statement concerning Senir "this signifies snow in the German language and in the Canaanite language" by drawing Tg. Onq.'s rendering into the discussion. They point out that the Targum probably followed some ancient tradition, one that also existed among the Arabs, for according to the Arab geographers the name for Mt. Hermon was *jébel ṯalǧ* ("snow-mountain"). Thus Rashi's explanation of Senir must be considered to be based on an ancient tradition common to the Hebrews and the Arabs. Indo-European linguistic influences upon Palestine may have been derived by the Hittites, according to Rosenbaum and Silbermann, who were already settled there by the time that Abraham arrived. In view of the verse stating that this mountain was called Senir by the Amorites, they conjecture that some affinity probably existed between the Hittites and Amorites according to Ezek. 16:3-5 who says to Jerusalem: "The Amorite was your father, and your mother was a Hittite." Hence Senir was the Hittite name of this mountain and Scripture tells us that the Amorites called it by this name. Thus Senir is of Indo-European origin, allied to German "Schnee" and Slavonic "snih," the final *r* in Senir corresponding to the Indo-European suffix *-ro* (as suggested by M. Buttensweiser).

There is likewise a reference to Mt. Hermon as the "snow-mountain" in the following Midrash—Sifre on Numbers (*Bālāq* CXXXI, p. 170): "The Ammonites and the Moabites built for themselves (fortified) enclosures from Beth Yeshimoth (in the south on the NE tip of the Dead Sea) to the snow-mountain (in the north)."

plain and all of Gilead, as well as all of *Maṯnan*[1] as far as *Salkha*[f] and Edrei, the cities of Og's kingdom in *Maṯnan.*[1] 11. For only Og king of *Maṯnan*[1] was left of the remaining giants; here his bedstead was an iron bedstead. Is it not in Rabbah of the Ammonites? Nine cubits is its length and forty cubits is its width in *royal cubits.*[4] 12. Now this territory we took into possession at that time, from Aroer which is on *the*[g] Wadi of Arnon and half of the hill country of Gilead together with its cities, I assigned to *the tribe of*[5] Reuben and to *the tribe of*[5] Gad. 13. Whereas the rest of Gilead and all of *Maṯnan*[1]—the kingdom of Og—I assigned to the half-tribe of Manasseh, the entire district of *Trachonitis,*[2] all that part of *Maṯnan*[1] which is called Land of the Giants. 14. Jair, son of Manasseh, took the entire region of *Trachonitis*[2] as far as the border of Gishorah and *Aphkeros,* and he named it after himself, so that to this day *Maṯnan*[1] is <known as> Villages of Jair. 15. Now to Makhir I assigned Gilead. 16. Moreover, to *the tribe of*[5] Reuben and to *the tribe of*[5] Gad I assigned <the area> from Gilead as far as the Wadi of Arnon, the center of the wadi being *its*[h] border, and up to the Jubeka wadi—the border of the Ammonites. 17. Whereas the plain, the Jordan and *its*[h] border from *Genesserat*[6] as far as the Sea of the Plain—the Salt Sea—below the area of *the discharge*[7] *from the heights,*[8] eastward. 18. Then I commanded you at that time, saying, 'The Lord your God has given you this land as an inherited possession; you should cross over armed for war ahead of your Israelite brethren, all those armed for battle. 19. Except for your wives, and your children as well as your livestock—I know you have much livestock—they should stay in your cities, the ones I assigned to you, 20. until the Lord grants rest to your brethren as {He has} to you, and they too will take possession of the land that the Lord your God is giving *them*[i] on the other side of the Jordan; then each one may return to his inherited possession which I have assigned to him.' 21. Now Joshua I commanded at that time, saying, 'Your eyes have seen all that the Lord your God has done to these two kings, so the Lord will do to all the kingdoms which you will pass. 22. Do not be afraid of them, for the Lord your God—*His Memra*[9]—will *fight*[j] for you.' 23. Then I prayed before the Lord at that time, saying, 24. 'O Lord *God,*[k] You have begun to show to Your servant Your greatness and Your powerful hand, that You are God, Your *Shekhinah*[l] is in the heavens above and You rule over the *earth;*[m] there is none who can do Your deeds or mighty works. 25. Let me now cross over and see the good land that is on the other side of the Jordan, the good mountain and the *Temple.*[10]' 26. But *anger emanated from before*[11] the Lord against me on account of you and he did not *listen to me;*[12] moreover, the Lord said to me, 'You had enough; do not continue to speak any longer about this matter *before*[13] Me. 27. Go up to the top of *the heights*[8] and

Apparatus, Chapter 3 (Cont.)

[f] C and c have: "Salakh."

[g] A adds: "shore of," as do the Tgs. Ps.-Jon., Neof., the Syr., the LXX, the Vg., and the Sam. Heb., as well as the Sam. Tg. (J). The Hebrew has this addition—*śpt* in 2:36 above.

[h] G has: "the," as does the Hebrew, and A has: "the" in the following verse.

[i] j, c, and l have: "you," as is the *Sebirin* in the Hebrew.

[j] n adds: "the war."

[k] D has: "Lord."

[l] h adds: "dwells."

[m] D adds: "below."

[n] i_a has: "bring this people across."

Apparatus, Chapter 4

[a] k has the plural.

raise your eyes to the west and to the north, to the east and to the south, and see with your <own> eyes that you will not cross this Jordan. 28. Then issue orders to Joshua and encourage him and strengthen him, for it is he who will *cross before this people,*[n] and it is he who will help them take possession of the land that you see.' 29. So we stayed in the valley facing Beth Peor.

CHAPTER 4

1. So now, O Israel, listen to the decrees and laws that I am about to teach you, in order that you may live and enter and take possession of the land that the Lord, the God of your fathers, is giving you. 2. Do not add <anything> to the *word*[a] that I command

Notes, Chapter 3 (Cont.)

[4]The Hebrew has: "by the cubit of a man," which the Tg. here specifies to be that of a royal personage—Og, who, like other kings of his time, set the standard for the actual equivalence of a cubit. Naḥmanides points out that the Targum here understood Hebrew *'îš* as if it had the definite article, which would then refer to "*the* man," "i.e., the king, hence the translation *mlk* in the Targum. Tg. Neof. has "the cubit of the king" (*dmlk'*), whereas Tg. Ps.-Jon. has "his own cubit."

[5]An insertion, implied in the Hebrew, to conform with vs. 13 where the term tribe occurs with the Manassites. Tgs. Ps.-Jon. and Neof. also have it, the latter even extending it as "the tribe of the descendants of."

[6]The Hebrew "Kinneret" is here translated by its appellation during the Talmudic period from the Greek *Γεννησαρέτ*.

[7]See Num. Chap. 21, n. 8.

[8]See *ibid.,* n. 15.

[9]See Introduction VII D. 1.

[10]The Hebrew has: "Lebanon," which the Targum here renders Temple in agreement with Rabbinic tradition set forth in the following texts:

1. *Sifre Wā'etḫannan* XXVIII, p. 45 "'and the Lebanon' (Deut. 3:25), from where (do we know) that Lebanon refers exclusively to (the) Temple as it says: (Jer. 22:6) 'you are Gilead unto me and the head of Lebanon,' 'and the Lebanon shall fall by a mighty one' (Isa. 10:34). (In Friedmann's edition [p. 71b]—'and Lebanon,' this refers to the Temple.) Now why was it called Lebanon? Because it makes white the sins of Israel, as it says: 'though your sins be as scarlet, they shall be as white as snow' (Isa. 1:18)."

2. *b. Yoma* 39b "Our Rabbis taught: 'During the last forty years before the destruction of the Temple . . . the doors of the *Hekal* would open themselves, until R. Joḥanan b. Zakkai rebuked them, saying: Why will you be the alarmer yourself. I know about you that you will be destroyed, for Zekhariah ben Ido has already prophesied concerning you: 'Open your doors, O Lebanon, that the fire may devour your cedars' (Zech. 11:1). R. Isaac b. Tablai said: Why is its name called Lebanon? Because it makes white the sins of Israel."

3. *b. Git.* 56b "'and the Lebanon shall fall by a mighty one' (Isa. 10:34) . . . Lebanon refers to the Temple, as it says 'this goodly mountain and Lebanon'" (referring back to the present verse).

Tg. Neof. has: "the Mount of the Temple," whereas Tg. Ps.-Jon. has: "the Mountain of Lebanon, on which the *Shekhina* is destined to dwell." Cf. further G. Vermes, "'Car le Liban, c'est le consil de la communaute': note sur Pésher d'Habacuc, 12, 3-4." *Melanges biblique.* Paris, 1957, pp. 316-25; and *idem,* "Lebanon" in *Scripture and Tradition in Judaism: Haggadic Studies.* Studia Post-Biblica IV. Leiden (E.J. Brill), 1961, pp. 26-39.

[11]See above Chap. 1, n. 18.

[12]See Gen. Chap. 16, n. 1.

[13]See Gen. Chap. 4, n. 1.

you, nor diminish <anything> from it, but observe the commandments of the Lord your God, that I command you this day. 3. Your eyes have seen what the Lord has done with the worshippers of Baal-Peor, for everyone who *followed*[b] Baal-Peor, the Lord your God has destroyed him from your midst. 4. But you who have cleaved to *the reverence of*[1] the Lord your God, all of you are {still} alive this day. 5. Realize that I have taught you decrees and laws as the Lord my God has commanded me, so that you may practice <them> accordingly in the midst of the land, which you are about to enter to take possession of it. 6. Now you should observe <them> and practice <them> for it will serve as your wisdom and discernment in the perception of the <other> nations, who will hear about all these decrees and will say, 'Surely, this great nation is a wise and discerning nation.' 7. For who is such a great nation *whose God is so close*[2] to it *to accept its prayer in time of its tribulation*[3] like the Lord our God whenever we *pray*[4] *before*[5] Him? 8. Moreover, who is such a great nation who has decrees and honest laws, as exemplified by this entire Law that I set before you this day? 9. Only be careful and watch yourselves exceedingly lest you forget the matters that your own eyes have seen, and lest they will pass from your heart all the days of your life; rather make them known to your children and your children's children. 10. The day you stood before the Lord your God at Ḥoreb, when the Lord said to me, Gather the people *before*[5] Me and I will let them hear My words, so that they learn *to act reverently before Me*[c] all the days that they live on earth, and so may teach their children. 11. So you approached and stood *at the foot of*[6] the mountain, while the mountain was ablaze with fire to the *very*[7] heavens <in > darkness and dense clouds. 12. Then the Lord spoke with you from the midst of the fire; you heard the sound of words, but you perceived no form, only a voice. 13. So He related to you His covenant which He commanded you to observe—the Ten Commandments—and He inscribed them on two tablets of stone. 14. At that time the Lord commanded me to teach you the decrees and the laws, for you to observe them in the land which you are about to cross into, in order to take possession of it. 15. Watch yourselves exceedingly, since you saw no form the day that the Lord spoke with you at Ḥoreb from the midst of the fire. 16. Lest you become corrupt and make for yourselves an image in the form of any shape, whether formed in the likeness of man or woman, 17. the form of any animal on earth, the form of any winged bird that flies in *the atmosphere of the expanse of*[8] the sky, 18. the form of anything that crawls on the ground, the form of any fish that is in the waters below the earth. 19. Lest you raise your eyes to the sky, and see the sun and the moon and the stars, all the hosts of heaven, and you will go astray and bow down to them and worship them—these which the Lord your God has designated <them to serve> all nations that are under the entire heavens. 20. Moreover, you the Lord has *brought close*[9] *to His reverence,*[1] and you He has brought out from the iron blast furnace that is Egypt, to be His {own} people, *His*[10] possession as you now are. 21. *Now anger emanated from before the Lord*[11] against me on your account, and He swore that I would not cross the Jordan, that I would not enter the good land, that the Lord your God giving you as an inherited possession. 22. For I am to die in this land, I am not to cross the Jordan, but you will cross and will take

Apparatus, Chapter 4 (Cont.)

[b] D adds: "the worship of."

[c] n has: "to revere Me," as does the Hebrew.

[d] D has: "exile."

possession of this land. 23. Watch yourselves, lest you forget the covenant of the Lord your God which He has established with you, and you will make for yourselves an image of any form, against which the Lord your God has enjoined you. 24. For the Lord your God *His Memra*[12] is an all-consuming fire; He is a jealous God. 25. When you have begotten children and grandchildren and have been in the land for a long time, if you should then become corrupt and make an image of any form and act wickedly before the Lord your God to provoke Him to anger, 26. I call heaven and earth to be witness against you this day, that you will surely perish quickly from the land into which you are about to cross the Jordan to take possession of it; you will not prolong <your> days on it, for you will summarily be destroyed. 27. Then the Lord will scatter you among the nations, and you will remain a numbered few people among the nations, where the Lord will *lead*[d] you. 28. There you will serve *the nations who worship*[13] idols, the product of

Notes, Chapter 4

[1]This insertion was meant to avoid the notion of man adhering to God, as expressed in the following Rabbinic discussion—

b. Ket. IIIb "'But you who cleave unto the Lord your God are alive, everyone of you this day' (Deut. 4:4). Now is it possible to cleave to the divine presence concerning which it is written in Scripture: 'For the Lord your God is a devouring fire' (*ibid.* 24)." Accordingly the Targum inserts *dḥlt'*—"the reverence of" to which man cleaves, to which man is "brought close" (vs. 20 below), which man "seeks" (vs. 29 below), to which man "returns" (vs. 30 below). It is also employed as an insertion whenever man is depicted as walking with God (cf. Gen. 5:22, 24 in the case of Enoch, and 6:9 in the case of Noah), or in a warning against man "forgetting" God (Deut. 6:12; 8:11, 14, 19). Tg. Ps.-Jon. renders similarly while Tg. Neof. inserts "the teaching of the Law."

[2]The Hebrew *'ělōhîm qrōḇîm* contains the difficult plural of the second term, a fact which was already noted in the following Talmudic passage—b. Sanh. 38b: "Said R. Joḥanan—Wherever (in a Biblical passage) the heretics seem to find a support for their scepticism (believe in a plurality of divine beings), their refutation is always near by, 'for what nation (is there so) great that has God so near to it, as the Lord our God is in all (things that) we call upon *him* (for)' (Deut. 4:7)." Thus the Targum, who renders the Hebrew *qrōḇîm* plural into a singular *qārēb* (as do Tgs. Ps.-Jon., Neof., the Frg. Tg. [V], the LXX, and the Syr.) runs parallel to the Rabbinic interpretation of this passage. The Sam. Tg. (J) and the Vg., however, render the verb in the plural.

[3]This addition complements the preceding clause by explaining in what way is God so close to the people; it also anticipates what follows ... "whenever we pray to Him." This motif occurs in Ps. 20:2 where the Hebrew "may the Lord answer you on the day of tribulation" is rendered there by the Tg. "may He accept your prayer."

[4]See Gen. Chap. 12, n. 7.

[5]See Gen. Chap. 4, n. 1.

[6]See Exod. Chap. 19, n. 12.

[7]The Targum employs the versatile particle *ṣēt,* here to avoid the figure of speech "heart (of the heavens)" in the Hebrew. Tgs. Neof. and Ps.-Jon. render similarly.

[8]An insertion implied in the Hebrew here, though partially present in Gen. 1:20 "and fowl that may fly above the earth in the open *expanse of* the heavens." Tg. Ps.-Jon. renders similarly, while Tg. Neof. only partially—"in the atmosphere of the sky."

[9]See Gen. Chap. 15, n. 7.

[10]Lit. "a."

[11]See above Chap. 1, n. 18.

[12]See Introduction VII D. 1.

[13]This insertion changes the thought of this passage, which according to the Hebrew says that in exile, Israel will worship idols, whereas according to the Targum, Israel will serve only the nations among whom it is scattered, but it is really the nations who are the ones who worship idols. This same situation exists below in 28:36. Y. Koraḥ (*Marpe Lashon* in *Sefer Keter Tora: Ha-Ta'ağ Ha-Gadol.* Jerusalem, 1960, on this verse)

human hands, of wood and of stone which cannot see, nor can hear, nor can eat, nor can smell. 29. From there if you will see *the reverence of*[1] the Lord your God, then you will indeed find <*Him*>,[14] if you will seek *before*[e] Him with all your heart and with all your soul. 30. Now when you will be in distress, and all these things will happen to you in later days, then you should return to *the reverence of*[1] the Lord your God and listen to *His Memra.*[12] 31. For the Lord your God is a God of mercy; He will not abandon you nor will He destroy you, nor will *the covenant of your ancestors be forgotten*[f] which He confirmed by oath to them. 32. If you would now ask about the former days which came before you, ever since the Lord created man on earth, from one end of heaven to the other <end of heaven>: Has there ever happened such a great thing, or has anything like it ever been heard? 33. Has any nation ever heard the voice of *the Memra of*[12] the Lord speaking from the midst of a fire as you have heard and survived? 34. Or has the Lord ever performed miracles *to reveal Himself*[15] so as to *redeem*[16] for Himself one nation from the midst of another nation with miracles, with signs, and with wonders, with battle, with a powerful hand, with a raised arm, and with a great visions, like all the things which the Lord did for you in Egypt before *your*[g] very eyes? 35. You were shown in order to realize that it is the Lord who is God; there is none beside Him. 36. From the heavens He let you hear *the voice of His Memra*[12] to train you, and on earth He showed you His great fire, while you heard His words from the midst of the fire. 37. Only because He loved your ancestors and delighted in their descendants after them, and brought you out of Egypt *with His Memra*[12] by His great strength, 38. to expel before you nations more numerous and more powerful than you, so as to bring you into their land and to give it to you as an inherited possession, as it is this day. 39. Now you should acknowledge this day and reflect <about it> in your heart, that the *Lord*[h] He is God, whose *Shekhinah*[17] *is*[i] in heaven above, and *who rules*[j] over the earth below; there is no one *else.*[k] 40. Moreover, you should observe His decrees and His commandments, which I command you this day, that it may go well with you and your descendants after you, and that you prolong <your> days in the land that the Lord your God is giving you for all time. 41. Then Moses set aside three cities on the <other> side of the Jordan *towards*[l] the sunrise. 42. where a manslayer could flee who had killed his fellowman without forethought, and without previously having had enmity towards him; now he could flee to one of these following cities and survive. 43. Bezer in the wilderness in the area of the plains, belonging to *the tribe of*[18] Reuben; Ramoth in Gilead, belonging to *the tribe of*[18] Gad; and Golan in *Maṯnan,*[19] belonging to *the tribe of*[18] Manasseh." 44. This is the Law that Moses set before the Israelites. 45. These are the testimonies,

Apparatus, Chapter 4 (Cont.)

[e] D and g omit, thus translating the Hebrew literally without the use of the buffer particle *qdm*.

[f] D and g have: "He will not forget the covenant of your ancestors," as does the Hebrew.

[g] Plural, whereas D has the singular, as does the Hebrew.

[h] l adds: "your God."

[i] h has: "dwells."

[j] D omits; the Hebrew does not have it.

[k] g adds: "beside Him," as in the Hebrew of vs. 35 above.

[l] D has: "from," adding an *m* prefix that could have dropped out via haplography.

[m] D has: "killed."

Apparatus, Chapter 5

[a] i_a has the literal: "in your ears."

[b] So also B, P, j, c, and d, whereas Sperber's main text has the plural, as does the Sam. Heb.

and the decrees, as well as the laws that Moses told the Israelites, after they departed from Egypt. 46. On this side of the Jordan, in the valley near Beth Peor, in the land of Siḥon, king of Amorites, who dwelt in Ḥeshbon, whom Moses and the Israelites *defeated*[m] after they had left Egypt. 47. They had taken possession of his land and of the land of Og, king of *Maṯnan,*[19] the two Amorite kings on this side of the Jordan *towards*[1] the sunrise. 48. From Aroer which is on the banks of the Wadi of Arnon, as far as Mount Sion, that is Hermon, 49. as well as the entire plain on the east side of the Jordan, as far as the sea of the plain below the area of the *discharge*[20] from *the heights.*[21]

CHAPTER 5

1. Then Moses summoned all of the Israelites and said to them, "Hear, O Israel, the decrees and the laws which I speak *before you*[a] this day, study them, and follow them diligently. 2. The Lord our God established a covenant with us at Ḥoreb. 3. Not merely with our ancestors did the Lord establish this covenant, but with us, all of us, those who are alive here this day. 4. *Literally*[1] did the Lord speak with you on the mountain from the midst of the fire. 5. I stood between *the Memra of*[2] the Lord and (between) you at that time to relate to you the *word*[b] of the Lord for you were afraid from before the fire, so you did not ascend the mountain—saying, 6. 'I am the Lord your God, who brought you out of the land of Egypt, out of the place of slavery. 7. You should have no other *god*[3] beside Me. 8. Do not make for yourself an image of any likeness <of anything> that is in the heavens above or <of anything> that is on earth below or <of anything>

Notes, Chapter 4 (Cont.)

explains that the Targum was forced into this interpretive translation because of the following verse "and from there you will seek the Lord your God . . ." which would be in direct contradiction to what preceeded if vs. 28 is rendered literally that they would be steeped in idolatry. Rashi expands on the Targum here—"for since you serve them (idols) it will be as though you served them."

[14]The Sam. Heb. and the Vg. actually have the 3rd. pers. sing. masc. pronominal suffix here.

[15]See Exod. Chap. 20, n. 10.

[16]The Hebrew has: "take" which is vague and accordingly rendered by the more definitive "redeem." Likewise, the Pal. Tgs., none of which render "take" literally—Tg. Ps.-Jon. having "separate (for Himself)," Tg. Neof. and the Frg. Tg. having "select (for Himself)."

[17]See Introduction VII D. 3.

[18]See above Chap. 3, n. 5.

[19]See Num. Chap. 21, n. 23.

[20]See Num. Chap. 21, n. 8.

[21]See *ibid.,* n. 15.

Notes, Chapter 5

[1]See Exod. Chap. 33, n. 7.

[2]See Introduction VII D. 1.

[3]Exod. Chap. 20, n. 1.

that is in the waters below the earth. 9. Do not bow down to them nor worship them, for I the Lord your God am a jealous God, avenging the sins of the fathers upon the *rebellious*[4] children, upon the third *generation*[5] and upon the fourth *generation*[5] of those who hate Me, when the children follow *their fathers*[c] *in sinning.*[6] 10. But performing kindness to thousands of *generations*[5] of those who love Me, and observe My commandments. 11. Do not *swear*[7] in vain with the name of the Lord your God, for the Lord will not acquit the one *who swears*[7] *falsely with His name.*[8] 12. Observe the Sabbath day by sanctifying it, as the Lord your God commanded you. 13. Six days you shall labor and perform all your work. 14. But the seventh day is a Sabbath to the Lord your God; <on it> you shall not perform any work—you, your son, your daughter, your servant, your maid, your ox, your donkey, and all your beasts, as well as your alien who is in your *city,*[9] so that your servant and maid may rest as you do. 15. Moreover, you should remember that you were a slave in the land of Egypt and the Lord your God brought you out from there with a mighty hand and a raised arm; therefore the Lord your God has commanded you to observe the Sabbath day. 16. Honor your father and your mother as the Lord your God has commanded you, so that your days may be prolonged, and so that you may fare well in the land which the Lord your God is giving you. 17. Do not kill *any person.*[10] 18. Do not commit adultery. 19. Do not *steal.*[d] 20. Do not *render false testimony*[e] against your fellowman. 21. (18) Do not lust after the wife of your fellowman, nor envy the house of your fellowman, <nor> his field, nor his servant, nor his maid, nor his ox, nor his donkey, nor anything that belongs to your fellowman.' 22. (19) These words the Lord spoke to your entire assembly on the mountain out of the fire and very dense clouds, a mighty voice without *ceasing;*[11] He then inscribed them on two tablets of stone and gave them to me. 23. (20) When you heard the voice out of the darkness, while the mountain was ablaze with fire, you approached me, all your tribal heads and your elders. 24. (21) Then you said, 'Here the Lord our God has shown us His glory and His dignity, while we heard *the voice of His Memra*[12] out of the fire; this day we realized that man can live even if God has spoken to him. 25. (22) So now, why should we die, since this great fire may consume us; if we continue to further hear the voice of *the Memra of*[2] the Lord our God, we shall die. 26. (23) For what mortal has ever heard the voice of *the Memra of*[2] the living Lord, speaking out of the fire as we did, and still survive? 27. (24) You approach and hear all that the Lord our God says; then you shall tell us all that the Lord our God told you, and we will accept and do. 28. (25) Then the tone of your words *were heard before the Lord*[13] as you spoke with me'; and the Lord said to me, 'The tone of the words of this people *was heard before Me*[13] as they spoke with you, everything they said is correct. 29. (26) O that they would have the heart to *show reverence before Me*[f] and to observe all My commandments at all times, so that

Apparatus, Chapter 5 (Cont.)

[c] D has: "father's faults."
[d] s adds: "any person," as does l in Exod. 20:13, for which see there Apparatus of Chap. 20, note *b*.
[e] D has: "act as a false witness."
[f] D has: "show Me reverence."
[g] D has: "possess."

Apparatus, Chapter 6

[a] c adds: "them."
[b] D has: "revere," as does the Hebrew.
[c] l has: "increase."
[d] k has: "accept."

they and their descendants would forever fare well. 30. (27) Go, say to them: Return to your tents. 31. (28) But you stand here before Me, and I will tell you the entire commandment, the decrees, as well as the laws, which you should teach them, that they may observe <them> in the land, which I am giving them as an inheritance. 32. (29) Now you should be observant in doing just as the Lord your God has commanded you; do not digress to the right or to the left. 33. (30) You should walk only on that path that the Lord your God has commanded you, so that you may live and fare well and prolong your days in the land that you will *inherit.*[g]'

CHAPTER 6

1. Now this is the command, the decrees, and the laws that the Lord your God has commanded {me} to teach you to *observe*[a] in the land, into which you are about to cross to inherit it, 2. so that you, your son, and your son's son will *show reverence before*[b] the Lord your God to observe all of his decrees and (His) commandments which I command you, (and) so that you will *prolong*[c] your days. 3. Moreover, accept O Israel and be observant in following through, so that you may fare well and increase exceedingly <in the> land *producing*[1] milk and honey, as the Lord, the God of your ancestors spoke to you. 4. *Hear*[d] O Israel, the Lord is our God, the Lord is one. 5. Now you should love the

Notes, Chapter 5 (Cont.)

[4]See *ibid.*, n. 2.
[5]See *ibid.*, n. 3.
[6]See *ibid.*, n. 4.
[7]See *ibid.*, n. 5.
[8]See *ibid.*, n. 6.
[9]See Gen. Chap. 22, n. 13.
[10]See *ibid.*, n. 7.
[11]The Hebrew has: "and He added no more." The Targum here renders this phrase interpretively to mean without pausing, i.e., He did not cease, in agreement with the following discussion in the Talmud where the present verse is linked to Num. 11:25 containing the identical expression with regards to Eldad and Medad—b. Sanh. 17a: "The Master said: All the other prophets prophesied and ceased, but they (the seventy elders) prophesied and did not *cease*. Whence do we infer that the others ceased? Shall we say, from the verse (Num. 11:25) 'They prophesied *wĕlo yāsāp̱û'* ('but they did not continue'). If so, what of the passage 'with a mighty voice *wĕlo yāsāp'*(Deut. 5:22). Does that too mean, 'it did not continue'? Rather the latter must be interpreted *'it did not cease.'* But here it is written ' and they prophesied' (Num. 11:25), whereas there (in the case of Eldad and Medad—Num. 11:27) it is stated 'they *were prophesying*, i.e., they were still continuing to prophesy." Cf. further b. Sot. 10b. Tg. Ps.-Jon., Tg. Neof., and CTgD render similarly, while the Syr. paraphrases "which cannot be measured."
[12]The Hebrew has: "His voice," for which cf. Introduction VII D. 1.
[13]See Gen. Chap. 29, n. 9.

Notes, Chapter 6

[1]See Exod. Chap. 3, n. 12.

Lord your God with your whole heart, and (with your whole) soul, as well as with all your *possessions.*[2] 6. Moreover, these words which I command you this day you should take to heart. 7. Then you should teach them to your children, by talking about them when you stay at home, and when you go on the road, as well as when you lie down and when you get up. 8. Now you should tie them as a sign on your hand and they should be in the form of *phylacteries*[3] between your eyes, 9. and you should inscribe them *in Mezuzot and affix them*[4] on the doorposts of your houses and of your gates. 10. When the Lord your God will bring you into the land which He swore to your ancestors—(to) Abraham, (to) Isaac, and (to) Jacob, to give you—great and flourishing cities which you did not build, 11. houses full of good things which you did not fill, hewn cisterns which you did not hew, vineyards and olive groves which you did not plant; then when you will eat and be satisfied, 12. watch yourself, lest you forget *the reverence of*[5] the Lord who brought you out of the land of Egypt from the place of slavery. 13. You should *show reverence to*[5] the Lord your God, and worship *before*[6] Him, as well as swear by His name. 14. Do not follow *the idols of the nations,*[7] any of the idols of the nations around you. 15. For the Lord your God is a jealous God, His *Shekhinah*[8] *is*[e] among you, lest you will arouse the anger of the Lord your God against you, then He will destroy you from the face of the earth. 16. Do not test *before*[f] the Lord your God as you tested <Him> at *Nisetha.*[9] 17. You should diligently observe the commandments of the Lord your God, and His testimonies, as well as His decrees which He commanded you. 18. Moreover, you should do what is proper and right before the Lord, so that you will fare well and enter and take possession of the good land that the Lord promised on oath to your ancestors, 19. to *shatter*[10] all your enemies before you, as the Lord has spoken. 20. When your son will ask you *in the future:*[11] 'What is <the meaning of> the testimonies, and decrees, as well as the laws that the Lord our God has commanded you,' 21. you should say to your son, 'We were slaves to the Pharaoh in Egypt, and the Lord brought us out of Egypt with a mighty hand! 22. Moreover, the Lord *sent*[12] great and terrible signs and wonders upon Egypt, on the Pharoah, and on all the members of his household, before our <very> eyes. 23. But us He brought out from there to give us the land which He promised on oath to our ancestors.' 24. Now the Lord commanded us to obey all these decrees to *show reverence before*[b] the Lord our God, so that we will fare well all the days, to preserve us as is the case this day. 25. It will therefore be to our merit that we be observant in following all of this precept before the Lord our God, as He commanded us.

Apparatus, Chapter 6 (Cont.)

[e] D has: "dwells."

[f] D and g omit; the Hebrew does not have it.

Apparatus, Chapter 7

[a] So also Y, G, O, and c, whereas Sperber's main text has: "revering."

Notes, Chapter 6 (Cont.)

[2]The Hebrew has: "might," which the Targum here renders in agreement with the Rabbinic interpretation to mean "possessions," "wealth," "money." Rabbi Eliezer states the opinion in the following Midrash—Sifre

CHAPTER 7

1. When the Lord your God will bring you into the land that you are about to enter, and take possession of it, He will expel many nations before you—the Hittites, the Girgashites, and the Amorites, as well as the Canaanites, (and) the Perizzites and the Hivites, as well as the Jebusites—seven nations who are more numerous and powerful than you. 2. But the Lord your God will deliver them before you, and you will defeat them; you must thoroughly put an end to them; do not establish any treaty with them, nor have *mercy*[1] on them. 3. You should not intermarry with them—you should not give your daughter to their son, nor take his daughter for your son, 4. for they will turn your children away from *worshiping*[a2] Me to worship *the idols of the nations,*[3] whereupon the

Notes, Chapter 6 (Cont.)

Wä'ethannan XXXII, p. 55 and *b. Ber.* 61b "If it says 'with all your soul' why should it also say 'with all your might,' and if it says 'with all your might' why should it also say 'with all your soul'? Should there be a man who values his life more than his money, for him it says: "with all your soul,' and should there be a man who values his money more than his life, for him it says: 'with all your might.'" Rabbi Eliezer's interpretation exists also in identical form in the following Talmudic tractates: b. Pes. 25a; b. Yoma 82a; and b. Sanh. 74a. Tgs. Ps.-Jon. and Neof. have specifically "money" (*mmwnkwn*) whereas the Syr. *qnynk* "acquisitions," is similar to Tg. Onq. The LXX (*καὶ ἐξ ὅλης τῆς δυνάμεώς σου* "with all your strength) and the Vg. (*et ex tota fortitudine tua* "with all your might") are literal. Cf. especially m. Ber. IX:5—"'with all your might'" (Deut. 6:5) means with all your money."

[3]See Exod. Chap. 13, n. 7, as well as Sifre *ibid.*, XXXV, p. 63f.

[4]An insertion, also in Tgs. Ps.-Jon., and Tg. Neof., according to which the inscription is not to be made on the doorposts themselves, but on parchment placed into a container, together known as Mezuza, which is the element that is affixed to the doorpost. This interpretation is in agreement with the following Rabbinic opinion concerning the meaning of this verse—

b. Men. 34a "R. Aḥa b. Raba said to R. Ashi: But the Divine Law says 'upon the doorposts' (Deut. 6:9, which would imply that it was actually written upon the wood) and you say we must infer the 'writing' here from the 'writing' there (that it should be written on a scroll)! (He replied,) The verse says: 'and you shall write' (Deut. 6:9) which implies a perfect writing (and this is the case only when writing is applied with ink upon a scroll, whereas any writing with ink upon wood or stones would be imperfect and indistinct), and then (place it) 'upon the doorposts.' But since then it is written: 'and you shall write them' (signifying that the writing must be upon a scroll) why do I need the analogy of the common expressions? Without the analogy I would have thought that one must write it upon a stone (i.e., carve the words upon a stone, which would qualify for a perfect and distinct writing), and set it up upon the threshold (as the doorpost), it therefore teaches otherwise." Cf. likewise Sifre *ibid.* XXXVI, p. 66 where a similar discussion occurs.

[5]See above Chap. 4, n. 1.

[6]See Gen. Chap. 4, n. 1.

[7]The Hebrew "other gods," for which see Introduction VII A.3.

[8]See Introduction VII D. 3.

[9]See Exod. Chap. 17, n. 4.

[10]See Lev. Chap. 26, n. 16.

[11]Lit. "tomorrow."

[12]Lit. "gave."

Notes, Chapter 7

[1]See Gen. Chap. 6, n. 8.

[2]See Num. Chap. 14, n. 24.

[3]See Introduction VII A.3.

anger of the Lord will be aroused against you, and it will summarily destroy you. 5. Rather you should do the following to them: Tear down their altars, smash their statues, cut down their Asherah poles, and burn *their images*[b] in fire. 6. For you are a sacred nation before the Lord your God; the Lord your God chose you to be His people, more beloved than any other nation {that is} on the face of the earth. 7. Not because you are the most numerous of all the nations did the Lord desire you and choose you; in fact you are the fewest of all the nations. 8. Rather it was because the Lord loved you and kept His oath which He promised to your ancestors, that the Lord brought you out with a mighty hand, and redeemed you from the place of slavery, from the power of the Pharaoh, king of Egypt. 9. Now you should realize that the Lord your God, it is He who is God, a trustworthy God, who keeps a generous covenant to those who love Him, and to those who keep His commandments to a thousand generations. 10. But He repays to those who hate Him *the good that they have done before Him*[4] *during their lifetime*[c] <eventually> to destroy *them;*[5] He does not delay *in being good*[4] to those who hate Him—*the good that they did before Him*[4] during their lifetime He will repay *them.*[5] 11. Now you should diligently follow the precept, and the decrees, as well as the laws which I command you this day. 12. Moreover, if you will obey these laws and diligently follow them, in exchange the Lord your God will follow through *for you*[d] on a generous covenant which He promised on oath to your ancestors, 13. and He will love you and He will bless you, as well as make you numerous and bless the *offspring*[6] of your womb and the fruit of your land, as well as your grain and your wine, and your oil, the offspring of your herds, and the breeds of your flocks, in the land which He promised on oath to give to you. 14. You shall be blessed above all nations; there shall be no sterile male or female among you or among your livestock. 15. The Lord will ward off from you all misfortunes; He will not put you through any of the dreadful diseases of *Egypt*[e] with which you are familiar, but will inflict them upon all your enemies. 16. Then you should *put an end to*[7] all the nations which the Lord your God delivers to you; do not have mercy on them, nor worship their *idols,*[3] for *they will be*[f] a trap to you. 17. Now *if*[g] you should say to yourselves, 'These nations are more numerous than I; how then will I be able to expel them?' 18. Do not be afraid of them; you shall surely remember that which the Lord your God did to the Pharoah and to all *the Egyptians:*[h] 19. The great miracles which your very eyes have seen, the signs and wonders, as well as the mighty hand and raised arm, by which the Lord your God brought you out, the Lord your God will do likewise to all the nations whom you <now> fear. 20. Furthermore, the Lord your God will also incite the hornet against them, until those who remain and hide from you will perish. 21. Do not be discouraged because of them, for the Lord your God, His *Shekhinah*[8] is in your midst, a great and awesome God. 22. Then the Lord your God will expel these nations before you little by little; you will not be able to destroy them summarily, lest the wild beasts will multiply against you. 23. Moreover, the Lord your

Apparatus, Chapter 7 (Cont.)

[b] D and i have: "the images of their idols."

[c] c omits.

[d] So also Y, B, M, and b, whereas Sperber's main text omits it.

[e] D and G have: "the Egyptians."

[f] A has: "they are," while D has: "it is," as does the Hebrew.

[g] M, b, and *d have: "perhaps," which is interpretive. (Vat. 448 has it in the margin.)

[h] So also b and g, whereas Sperber's main text has: "Egypt."

God will deliver them before you, and He will throw them into utter chaos, until they are destroyed. 24. He will then deliver their kings into your hand, and you shall eliminate their name from under the heavens; no person shall stand up before you, until you have destroyed them. 25. You should burn their images in fire; do not covet the silver and gold that they have on them, then taking <it> for yourself, lest you be trapped by it; for it is abominable before the Lord your God. 26. Nor should you bring that which is abominable into your house or you will be proscribed like it; you should utterly despise it and utterly remove it, for it is proscribed.

CHAPTER 8

1. Every command that I give you this day you should diligently follow, in order that you may live and increase, and enter and take possession of the land, that the Lord promised on oath to your ancestors. 2. Now you should remember the entire journey on which the Lord your God led you these forty years in the wilderness, in order to afflict

Notes, Chapter 7 (Cont.)

[4]These additions in the Targum for one were meant to supply direct object clauses for the verb involved and essentially reflect the widespread Rabbinic notion that God promptly repays the wicked in this world for any good they accomplish in order to eventually destroy them from this world and especially from the future world. This view is expressed in the following Rabbinic texts:

1. Tanḥ(A) *Ki Tissā'* XXVII; Tanḥ(B) *Ki Tissā'* XVI, p. 116 and Exod. Rab. XLV:5 "... The expression 'My face' (Exod. 32:20) here means the prosperity of the wicked, as it is written 'and repays them that hate Him to their face, to destroy them' (Deut. 7:10)."

2. *Shoḥ. Tob.* VII:17, p. 70 "... nevertheless the Prophets asked the Holy One, blessed be He: Why do You bestow worldly wealth upon the nations of the earth? God replied: Have I not told you in Scripture that 'the Lord your God ... repays them that hate Him to their face to destroy them' (Deut. 7:10)" i.e, God rewards the wicked for their good deeds in this world."

ibid. XCIV:4, p. 418 "... but the reward of the wicked is paid them here and now, as it is said: 'God ... repays them that hate Him to their face, to destroy them' (Deut. 7:10)."

3. *PRK* XXV *Šûḇāh*, p. 161b "... but He bestows tranquility in abundance upon the wicked in this world, thereby rewarding them in this world for their few good deeds, in order to requite them in full in the world to come, as it says: 'and He repays to those who hate Him to their face to destroy them, He does not delay ...' (Deut. 7:10)."

4. PXXIII *Yodh Haddibrôt* Iv, p. 124a "...the Holy One, blessed be He, does not delay in this world the reward of those among the heathen who do deeds of mercy. Of this reward it is written: 'and repays them that hate Him to their face' (Deut. 7:10)."

Cf. further on this subject, Ruth Zuta I:8 (ed. S. Buber, p. 42); Tanḥ(B) *Wayyiggaš* VIII, p. 207; Midrash Debarim Rabbah *Éqeb, op. cit.*, p. 74; and Otiyot de R. Aqiba Version A (in *Batei Midrashot.* Second edition, ed. A.J. Wertheimer. Jerusalem [Ktab Wasepher] 1968, p. 362).

[5]The Targum transforms the idiomatic singular "him" into a plural.

[6]See Gen. Chap. 30, n. 1.

[7]The idiomatic Hebrew "consume" is here accordingly rendered into its intended meaning. Tg. Ps.-Jon. renders identically.

[8]See Introduction VII D.3.

you so as to test *you,*[a] to know what was in your heart, whether you would keep His commandments or not. 3. So He afflicted you and caused you famine, then fed you the Manna, which neither you nor your ancestors had ever known, in order to make you aware that man does not live by bread alone, but man lives by everything that emanates from *the word of*[b] the Lord. 4. The clothes on you did not wear out, *nor did your sandals tear*[1] these forty years. 5. Now you should be aware in your heart that just as a man trains his son, so does the Lord your God train you. 6. Moreover you should observe the commandments of the Lord your God, *to follow the paths that are proper before Him,*[2] and to show reverence for Him. 7. For the Lord your God is bringing you into a good land, a land flowing with streams of water, fountain springs, and deep water pools emanating from valleys and hills. 8. A land of wheat and barley as well as vines, (and) figs and pomegranates; a land *whose olives produce oil, and it produces honey.*[3] 9. A land where you may eat bread without scarcity, <where> you will lack nothing; a land whose rocks are iron, and you can *mine*[4] copper from its hills. 10. When you have eaten to satisfaction, you should praise the Lord your God for the good land that He has given you. 11. Watch yourself lest you forget *the reverence for*[5] the Lord your God, *so as*[c] not to observe His commands and His laws as well as His decrees, which I command you this day. 12. When you have eaten to satisfaction and have built fine houses in which to live, 13. and your herds and your flocks have become *numerous*[d] and (your) silver and gold have increased for you, in fact everything that belongs to you has multiplied, 14. your heart might then grow haughty, and you might forget *the reverence for*[i] the Lord your God, who brought you out of the land of Egypt, out of the place of slavery, 15. who led you through this great and terrible wilderness, a place of fiery snakes and scorpions, an area of parched land with no water {in it}, who brought forth water for you from a *hard*[6] rock, 16. who fed you the Manna in the wilderness which your ancestors had never known, so as to afflict you in order to test you that you may ultimately fare well, 17. and you will say to yourselves: My own strength and the power of my own hand *have acquired*[e] these possessions for me. 18. Then you should *remember*[f] the Lord your God, that it was He who gave *you*[g] *advice*[h] how to acquire <these> posessions, in order to confirm His covenant that He swore to your ancestors, as it is this day. 19. Now if you will totally forget *the reverence for*[i5] the Lord your God, and follow *the idols of the nations,*[7] worshipping them and bowing down to them, I

Apparatus, Chapter 8

[a] i adds: "and in order."
[b] M omits.
[c] c omits.
[d] G adds: "for you."
[e] v has the singular form of the verb: "has acquired," as does the Hebrew, while b and g have: "has accumulated," and l adds: "all."
[f] l adds: "the reverence of."
[g] The text has *bk,* whereas G, i, c, k, and l have *lk,* as does the Hebrew.
[h] D has: "strength," as does the Hebrew.
[i] D omits.
[j] D has: "exile."
[k] The perfect, whereas i has: "would," the imperfect form, a literal rendering of the Hebrew.

Apparatus, Chapter 9

[a] D has: "expel." See above Chap. 2, n. 12 on this interchange.
[b] Sperber's main text has the plural, as does the Hebrew.
[c] G and V have the plural.

testify against you this day that you will surely perish, 20. like the nations that the Lord will *cause to perish*[j] before you, so will you perish, just because you *did*[k] not *accept*[8] the *Memra*[9] of the Lord your God.

CHAPTER 9

1. Hear, O Israel, you are {now} about to cross the Jordan to go in and *inherit*[a] nations more numerous and more powerful than you, great cities fortified {with walls} *towards*[1] the heavens. 2. A nation great and *strong,*[2] the descendants of the *giant,*[b] about whom you have been aware and about whom you have heard {it said}, 'Who can stand up against the descendants of the *giant*?!"[c] 3. You should realize now that the Lord your God will cross ahead of you; *His Memra*[3] is a consuming fire; He will destroy them, and

Notes, Chapter 8

[1]The Hebrew has: "nor did your feet swell." Adler (*Netina La-Ger* in *Sefer Torat Elohim.* Wilna, 1886, on this verse) explains this deviation in the Targum as an attempt on his part to retain the symbolism of the preceding clause which dealt with apparel, accordingly the parts of the body were here rendered by the apparel for these limbs. Löwenstein (*Nefesh Ha-Ger:* Deuteronomy. Pietrokov, 1912, p. 19f.) however, correctly points to Deut. 29:4 "your garment did not wear out from you, not did the sandal wear out from your foot," which obviously influenced the Targum to deviate from the text in the present verse. Tgs. Neof. and Ps.-Jon., as well as the Syr., paraphrase "your feet did not go bare."

[2]See Gen. Chap. 18, n. 8.

[3]The Hebrew "olive oil and honey" is concise and accordingly expanded "olive oil" to "olives *producing* oil," and "honey" to *producing* honey," as in the common expression "a land of milk and honey," which is rendered by the Targum" a land *producing* milk and honey," for which cf. Exod. Chap. 3, n. 13.

[4]Lit. "hew, carve."

[5]See above Chap. 4, n. 1.

[6]The Hebrew *ḥallāmîš* "flint" is here rendered by the adjective "hard" to reflect the Hebrew genitive phrase *ṣûr haḥallāmîš*. Since *ṣûr* ("rock") and *haḥallāmîš* are elsewhere used as synonyms, as in Ps. 114:8, the combination here suggests a hendiadys type of translation. The word occurs only five times in the entire Biblical text: In 32:13 below it is paraphrased; in Isa. 50:7 the Tg. Neb. renders it by the usual Aramaic equivalent *ṭynr* for Heb. *ṣwr* "rock;" and in Ps. 114:8; and Job 28:9 where it is rendered *šāmîr* "flint" by the Targum; in the former, *ṭynr* was used to translate Hebrew *ṣwr* the synonymous parallel item in the same verse, while in the latter *ṭynr* was used in the following verse for *ṣwr* similarly constituting a synonymous parallel to the preceding verse. The Tgs. Ps.-Jon. and Neof., however, employ the more literal combination *šāmîr tînārā'*, "rock of flintstone," as does the Syr. *k'p̱' dṭnr'* with the identical meaning.

[7]See Introduction VII A.3.

[8]See Gen. Chap. 16, n. 1.

[9]The anthropomorphic *qôl*—"voice" is here entirely replaced by the Memra, in contrast to Tg. Neof. here, where Memra is merely inserted after *ql* to become "the voice of the Memra," and Deut. 4:36; 5:24, as well as Gen. 3:10 where Tg. Onq. too merely inserts Memra.

Notes, Chapter 9

[1]See Gen. Chap. 11, n. 5.

[2]The Hebrew has: "tall," for which see Num. Chap. 24, n. 14.

[3]See Introduction VII D.1.

He will defeat them completely *from*[d] before you, so that you may expel them and summarily annihilate them, as the Lord has told you. 4. Do not say to yourself when the Lord will completely *shatter*[4] them before you, as follows: The Lord has brought me *in*[e] to take possession of this land on account of my merit, and on account of *the sins of*[5] these nations did the Lord expel them before you. 5. It is not on account of your merit, nor because of *your sincere integrity*[6] that you are coming {here} to take possession of this land, but rather because of *the sins of*[5] these nations did the Lord your God expel them before you, in order to fulfill the *promise*[7] which He swore to your ancestors—to Abraham, (to) Isaac, and to Jacob, 6. Now you should realize, that it is not because of your merit that the Lord your God is giving you this good land to possess, for you are a stiffnecked people. 7. Remember *never*[8] to forget how you provoked the Lord your God to anger in the wilderness, from the day that you departed from the land of Egypt until you came to this place, you have been rebellious *before*[9] the Lord. 8. Moreover, at Ḥoreb you provoked the Lord to anger, *and the anger of the Lord was aroused*[f] against you to destroy you. 9. When I ascended the mountain to receive the tablets of stone, the Tablets of the Covenant which the Lord had made with you, I stayed on the mountain {for} forty days and {for} forty nights, eating no bread and drinking no water. 10. Thereafter, the Lord gave me the two tablets of stone, inscribed by the finger of the Lord, and on them were *the exact*[10] words that the Lord had spoken to you on the mountain from the midst of the fire on the day of the assembly. 11. Then at the end of forty days and forty nights, the Lord gave me the two tablets of stone, the Tablets of the Covenant. 12. Whereupon the Lord said to me, 'Quickly, proceed to go down from here, for your people whom I brought out from Egypt have become corrupt; they quickly strayed from the path which I ordered them <to take>; they made for themselves a molten image.' 13. Then the Lord said to me as follows, '*It is revealed before Me*[11] about this people, that it is a stiffnecked people. 14. *Stop your prayer from before Me*[12] and I will destroy them and erase their name from beneath the heavens; thereafter I will make you into *a more powerful and more numerous*[g] nation than they.' 15. So I turned and descended from the mountain while the mountain was ablaze with fire, and the two Tablets of the Covenant were on my two hands. 16. Now I saw that you sinned before the Lord your God; you made for yourselves a molten image of a calf; you quickly strayed from the path that the Lord your God ordered you <to take>. 17. Whereupon I grasped the two Tablets, and flung them out of my two hands, smashing them before your eyes. 18. Then I fell prostrate before the Lord {for} forty days and {for} forty nights, as before; I did not eat bread nor did I drink water, because of all the sins that you committed, by acting wickedly before the Lord to provoke Him. 19. For I was afraid of the fierce anger, which the Lord directed against you with the intention of destroying you, but the Lord *accepted my prayer*[13] even at that time. 20. Moreover, *there was*[h] *excessive anger from before the Lord*[14] against Aaron with the intention of destroying him, but I prayed for Aaron as well at that time. 21. Now concerning that sinful thing

Apparatus, Chapter 9 (Cont.)

[d] So also C, whereas Sperber's main text omits it.
[e] D omits, using *'ṭy* in literal translation for Hebrew *bw'*.
[f] M has: "and there was anger from before the Lord."
[g] c reverses the order.
[h] d_1 adds: "also," perhaps influenced by the end of this verse.
[i] G adds: "the decree of."

you have made—the calf, I took it and burned it in the fire, and ground it thoroughly with a pestle until it became fine as dust; then I threw its dust into the stream that descends from the mountain. 22. Then at "Fire" and at *Nisetha,*[15] as well as at *Graves of the Demanders*[16] you provoked the Lord to anger. 23. And when the Lord sent you from *Reqem-Geah*[17] saying, 'Go up and take possession of the land which I am giving you,' you rebelled *against*[i] the *Memra*[18] of the Lord your God, and did not believe Him nor *accept His Memra.*[19] 24. You have been rebellious *before*[9] the Lord since the day I have known you. 25. When I fell prostrate before the Lord *those*[20] forty days and *those*[20] forty nights and lay prostrated, <it was> because the Lord had *intended*[21] to destroy you. 26. So I prayed before the Lord and said, 'O Lord God, do not destroy Your people and Your possession, which You redeemed with Your *power,*[22] and whom You brought out of Egypt with a powerful hand. 27. Remember your servants—Abraham, Isaac, and Jacob; do not pay attention to the stiffneckedness of this people or to their *faults*[23] and to their *sins,*[23] 28. lest the inhabitants of the land from which you brought them out will say: Because the Lord did not have the *power*[24] to bring them into the land which He

Notes, Chapter 9 (Cont.)

[4]See Lev. Chap. 26, n. 16.

[5]The Hebrew has: "wickedness," which the Targum, as well as the Tgs. Ps.-Jon. and Neof. and the Syr., renders "sins of." The deviation revolves around the logical association of the wicked ones and wickedness with sin, as is apparent in Prov. 13:6—"wickedness overthrows the sinner." In this vein the two terms become synonymous, resulting in the word "wickedness" here taking on the meaning of "sin," and consequently being pluralized by the Targum as standard procedure, for which see Gen. Chap. 21, n. 7. Cf. further Tg. Neb. to Ezek. 18:20; 33:12 and Mal. 3:15, 19 where Hebrew ***ršʿh*** ("wickedness") is rendered "sin" in the singular, and Isa. 9:17; Ezek. 18:27; 33:19 in the plural.

[6]Lit. "the honesty of your heart."

[7]Lit. "word."

[8]Lit. "do not."

[9]See Gen. Chap. 4, n. 1.

[10]Lit. "according to all."

[11]See Gen. Chap. 29, n. 8.

[12]See Exod. Chap. 32, n. 6 where a similar, though not identical expression occurs in the Hebrew ("let me alone"), and is likewise rendered by the Targum "stop your prayer from before Me."

[13]See Gen. Chap. 16, n. 1 and 5.

[14]See above Chap. 1, n. 18.

[15]See Exod. Chap. 17, n. 4.

[16]See Num. Chap. 11, n. 5.

[17]See Num. Chap. 32, n. 6.

[18]See Exod. Chap. 17, n. 1.

[19]See Gen. Chap. 22, n. 14.

[20]Lit. "the."

[21]Lit. "said."

[22]The Hebrew has: "greatness" which the Targum renders "power," perhaps as a result of an association with Neh. 1:10 where the subject matter is also "the Lord having redeemed" but there follow the words "with Your great power," as they do in vs. 29 below which may have figured in the association with the present verse and influenced the Targum to translate Hebrew *gdlk* here as "power." Tgs. Neof. and Ps.-Jon. render similarly here, as does the LXX which has ἐν τῇ ἰσχύι σου τῇ μεγάλῃ—"with your great power" (as in vs. 29 below).

[23]The Hebrew has: "his wickedness" and "his sin," which the Targum here pluralizes, rendering the first word interpretively, for which see n. 5 above.

[24]Lit. "capability."

promised them,[25] and because He hated them He brought them forth to kill them in the wilderness. 29. Now they are Your people and Your possession, whom you brought forth with Your great might and Your raised arm.'

CHAPTER 10

1. At that time the Lord said to me, 'Carve out two tablets of stone like the first ones, and come up *before*[1] Me on the mountain, and make for yourself a wooden ark. 2. Then I will inscribe on the tablets the words that were on the first tablets which you broke, then place them in the ark.' 3. So I made an ark of acacia wood and carved out two tablets of stone like the first ones, then I ascended the mountain with the two tablets in my hands. 4. Then He inscribed on the tablets the same text as on the first ones—the ten commandments, which the Lord spoke to you on the mountain from the midst of the fire on the day of the assembly, and the Lord gave them to me. 5. Whereupon I turned and descended from the mountain and placed the tablets into the ark which I had made; now there they remained, as the Lord had commanded me. 6. Then the Israelites set out from Beeroth-Bene-Jaakan to Mosera; there Aaron died and there he was buried, and Eleazar, his son, ministered in his place. 7. From there they set out for Gudgod, and from Gudgod to Jotbath, an area of running streams of water. 8. At that time the Lord set apart the tribe of Levi to carry the Ark of the Lord's Covenant, to stand <in attendance> before the Lord so as to serve Him and to bless in His name, as it is still this day. 9. Therefore, Levi did not have a part and an inheritance portion with his brothers; *the gifts which the Lord has given him,*[a] *they are*[b] his inheritance share, as the Lord your God has spoken concerning him. 10. Now I had stayed on the mountain forty days and forty nights as during *the earlier period,*[2] and the Lord *accepted my prayer*[3] this time as well, <since> the Lord does not want to destroy you. 11. Then the Lord said to me, 'Proceed to resume marching before the people, that they may enter and take possession of the land, which I swore to your ancestors to give them.' 12. So now O Israel, what does the Lord your God demand of you, except to *act reverentially before*[c] the Lord your God to follow *the proper paths before Him,*[4] to love Him, and to worship *before*[1] the Lord your God with all your heart and with all your soul. 13. To observe all the commandments of the Lord as well as His decrees, which I command you this day so that you may fare well. 14. Here, the heavens, even the highest heavens along with the

Apparatus, Chapter 10

[a] So also Y and T, whereas Sperber's main text has simply: "the Lord," as does the Hebrew.

[b] So also A, E, K, Y, k, and c, whereas Sperber's main text has: "it is," as does the Hebrew.

[c] D has: "to revere."

[d] So also Y and T, as well as the Hebrew, whereas Sperber's main text omits.

[e] d_2 and k have: "gods," as does the Hebrew.

[f] The form is plural (*mry*) but to be understood as *pluralis majestatis*. Yet k has the singular form (*mr'*), as do the Sam. Heb., the Sam. Tg. (J), and the Syr., as well as Tg. Neof., whereas Tg. Ps.-Jon. has the plural form.

earth and everything that is in them, belong to the Lord your God. 15. The Lord your God desired your ancestors exclusively, loving them and taking delight in their *descendants*[5] after them, *in you*[d] above all nations, as it is today. 16. Therefore, *remove the obduracy from your heart*[6] and do not stiffen your necks any longer. 17. For the Lord your God He is *the God of judges*[e] *and the Lord*[f] *of kings,*[7] a great God, mighty and awesome, who shows no favor and *accepts*[8] no bribes, 18. who *takes up*[9] the case of the orphan and widow, and loves the alien, providing him with food and clothing. 19. Now you should love the alien for you were alien residents in the land of Egypt. 20. You should revere the Lord your God, and worship *before*[1] Him; *stay close to His reverence,*[10] and swear by His name. 21. He is your glory and He is your God, who has done these great and mighty things for you, which your own eyes have seen. 22. Your ancestors descended into Egypt seventy persons in all, but now the Lord your God has made you as numerous as the stars of heaven.

CHAPTER 11

1. Now you should love the Lord your God and observe *the requirements of His Memra,*[1] and His decrees, as well as His laws, and His commandments always. 2. Moreover, you should realize this day, that it was not your children who have known

Notes, Chapter 9 (Cont.)

[25]Lit. "spoke to them."

Notes, Chapter 10

[1]See Gen. Chap. 4, n. 1.
[2]Lit. "the earlier days."
[3]See Gen. Chap. 16, n. 1 and 5.
[4]See Gen. Chap. 18, n. 8.
[5]See Gen. Chap. 3, n. 8.
[6]The Hebrew figure of speech "Circumcise the foreskin of your heart" is accordingly paraphrased with "circumcise" rendered "remove" as the act of circumcision involved the removal of the foreskin, and "foreskin" is rendered "obduracy." Similarly Tg. Ps.—Jon., whereas Tg. Neof. has the literal "circumcise" then follows it with both terms "foreskin" and "obduracy" in combination—"the foreskin of the obduracy of your heart." Tg. Neof. m. has "the hardness of your heart."
[7]The Hebrew has: "God of gods and Lord of lords." In order to avoid any sort of comparison between God and the gods of the nations, or between the Lord and other lords, the Targum renders "gods" as "judges" for which there is solid Biblical support (cf. Exod. 22:7, 8), and "lords" as "kings", as God is described as "King of kings" in Dan. 2:37. Tg Ps.-Jon. is identical to Tg. Onq. here, whereas the Syr., and the Sam. Tg. are literal. The text of Tg. Neof. at this point is questionable.
[8]See Gen. Chap. 4, n. 8.
[9]Lit. "does, makes."
[10]The Hebrew "cleave to Him" has anthropomorphic overtones and is accordingly paraphrased. Tg. Ps.-Jon. is identical here, where Tg. Neof. paraphrases "you should cleave to the teaching of His Law."

Notes, Chapter 11

[1]The Hebrew has: "His requirements." As the notion of "requirement" (Hebrew *mišméret*) is human in nature, the Targum accordingly paraphrases by inserting the Memra.

and perceived the lesson of the Lord your God, His majesty, His mighty hand and raised arm; 3. as well as His signs and His deeds which He performed in the midst of *Egypt*[a] against the Pharaoh, king of Egypt and (against) all of his land; 4. and what He did to the Egyptian army, to its horses and (to its) riders, when He caused the waters of the Sea of Reeds to overflow against them, when they were pursuing *you,*[b] and destroyed them *once and for all;*[2] 5. and what He did for you in the wilderness before you arrived in this place; 6. and what He did to Dathan and Abiram, sons of Eliab, the son of Reuben, when the earth opened its mouth and swallowed them up and the members of their household, as well as their tents and every living thing that belonged to them, in the midst of the Israelites. 7. Rather it was your <own> eyes that saw every great deed of the Lord, that He performed. 8. Now you should observe every commandment that I give you this day, so that you have the strength to enter and take possession of the land, into which you are now passing to inherit it. 9. Moreover, that you may prolong *<your>*[3] days in the land that the Lord swore to your ancestors to give to them and to their *descendants,*[4] a land *producing*[5] milk and honey. 10. For the land which you are about to enter and take possession of it, is unlike the land of Egypt from which you departed, where you *planted*[c] your seed and irrigated it by foot, like a vegetable garden. 11. Whereas the land into which you are about to cross and possess, is a land of hills and valleys, which *drinks*[d] its water from the rains of the heaven. 12. {It is} a land which the Lord your God looks after; *the eyes of*[6] the Lord your God are continually on it, from the beginning of the year to the end of the year. 13. If then, you will diligently *accept*[7] *My*[e] commandments which I give you this day to love the Lord your God and to worship Him with your whole heart and (with your whole) soul, 14. I will then grant rain for your land in its season, the early rain and the late (rain), and you will gather in your grain, and (your) wine, and (your) oil. 15. Moreover, I will provide grass in your field for your cattle, and you will eat and be satisfied. 16. Watch yourselves lest your hearts will stray, and you will be diverted into worshipping *the idols of the nations*[8] and bowing down to them. 17. Then the anger of the Lord will be aroused against you, and He will restrain the heavens so that there will be no rain, and the earth will not yield its produce; and you will soon perish from the good land that the Lord is giving you. 18. Now you should fix these words on your hearts and (on your) souls; and tie them as a sign on your hands and they should be in the form of *phylacteries*[9] between your eyes. 19. Moreover, you should teach them to your children, by talking about them when you stay at home, and when you go on the road, as well as when you lie down and when you get up; 20. and you should inscribe them in *Mezuzot and affix them*[10] on the doorposts of your houses and your gates. 21. So that your days and the days of your children will be many, in the land that the Lord your God swore to your ancestors to give to them, <as many> as the days that the heavens are above the earth. 22. If, then, you will

Apparatus, Chapter 11

[a] h and l have: "the Egyptians," as does a marginal variant.

[b] (d_2 = y) c and d have: "them," as do various Hebrew readings in Kennicott.

[c] So also D, b, and g, whereas J has: "would plant," as does the Hebrew.

[d] n has: "would drink," as does the Hebrew.

[e] l has: "the," as does the LXX.

[f] D omits.

[g] So also J and T, whereas Sperber's text has: "more numerous."

[h] i_a adds: "great," as do Cairo Geniza Hebrew fragments, the Tgs. Neof. and Ps.-Jon., the LXX, and the Vg.

[i] G has the literal: "hinder."

diligently observe this entire precept that I command you to do, to love the Lord your God, to follow *all*[f] *the paths that are proper before Him,*[11] *and to stay close to His reverence.*[12] 23. then the Lord will expel all these nations before you and will inherit nations *greater*[g] and more powerful than you. 24. Every place *where you set foot*[13] will be yours, from the wilderness to the Lebanon, from *the*[h] river—the Euphrates River to the *Western*[i] Sea, shall your territory *extend.*[14] 25. No man shall stand up to you; the Lord your God will put the fear (of you) and the terror of you on the face of the entire land *where you set foot,*[13] as the Lord told you. 26. Realize that I am setting before you this day *blessings*[15] and *curses,*[15] 27. *blessings,*[15] if you will *accept*[7] the commandments of the Lord your God, which I am giving you this day, 28. and *curses,*[15] if you will not *accept*[7] the commandments of the Lord your God, and turn away from the way which I command you this day, to follow the *idols of the nations*[8] which you have not *experienced.*[16] 29. When the Lord your God will bring you into the land that you are about to enter to take possession of it, then you shall place *those who <will> bless*[17] on Mount Gerizim *and those who <will> curse*[17] on Mount Ebal. 30. Are they not <both> on the other side of the Jordan, behind the road of the setting of the sun, in the land of the Canaanite who dwells in the plain, over against Gilgal on the side of the Plain of Moreh? 31. For you are about to cross the Jordan, to go in and take possession of the land that the Lord your God is giving you; when you have taken possession of it and dwell in it, 32. you should diligently follow all the decrees and all the laws that I have set before you this day.

Notes, Chapter 11 (Cont.)

[2]Lit. "until this day."

[3]The Qumran fragments actually have it.

[4]See Gen. Chap. 3, n. 8.

[5]See Exod. Chap. 3, n. 12.

[6]Oddly enough, the Targum does not circumvent this blatant anthropomorphism; neither do Tgs. Ps.-Jon. or Neof.

[7]See Gen. Chap. 16, n. 1.

[8]See Introduction VII A.3.

[9]See Exod. Chap. 13, n. 6.

[10]See above Chap. 6, n. 4.

[11]See Gen. Chap. 18, n. 8.

[12]See above Chap. 10, n. 10.

[13]Lit. "where the sole of your foot treads."

[14]Lit. "will be."

[15]See Gen. Chap. 21, n. 7.

[16]Lit. "known."

[17]The Hebrew has: "the blessing . . . the curse" which is a figure of speech to mean those who pronounce the blessings and those who pronounce the curses; the Targum paraphrases accordingly. The Tg. Ps.-Jon. does likewise within the context of his elaborate paraphrase here.

CHAPTER 12

1. These are the decrees and the laws which you should diligently follow, in the land that the Lord, the God of your ancestors, is giving you to possess, all the time that you are living in the land. 2. You shall utterly destroy all the places where the nations, whom you are dispossessing, worshipped their idols—on the high mountains, and on the hills, as well as under every leafy tree. 3. Now you should tear down their altars and smash their statues, as well as burn their sacred poles in fire; moreover, cut down the images of their idols and obliterate their name from that place. 4. But do not act likewise *before*[1] the Lord your God. 5. Rather <seek> only the place that the Lord your God will choose from among all your tribes to let His *Shekhinah*[2] dwell there as a site for His *Shekhinah,*[2] there you should *go,*[3] 6. and there you should bring your burnt offerings and your *sanctified sacrifices,*[4] as well as your tithes and your personal contribution, your votive offerings and your freewill offerings, as well as the firstborn of your herds and your flocks. 7. Moreover, there you and the member(s) of your households should eat and rejoice in all your undertakings, in which the Lord your God has blessed you. 8. Do not act as we now act here this day, every man *as he sees fit.*[5] 9. For you have not yet come to the resting place *of your*[6] inheritance, which the Lord your God is giving you. 10. But when you will cross the Jordan and settle in the land that the Lord your God is giving you as an inheritance, He will give you rest from all your enemies around you, and you will dwell in security. 11. Now the place that the Lord your God will choose to let His *Shekhinah*[2] dwell there, there you should bring all that I command you—your burnt offerings and your *sanctified sacrifices,*[4] your tithes and your personal contributions, as well as the choicest of your votive offerings that you will vow *before*[1] the Lord. 12. Then you should rejoice before the Lord your God, you and your sons and your daughters, as well as your servants and your maids and the Levite of your city, for he has no inherited portion among you. 13. Watch yourself lest you offer up your burnt offerings anywhere you see fit. 14. Rather, only in the place which the Lord will choose from one of your tribes, there you should sacrifice your burnt offerings, and there you should observe everything that I command you. 15. Nevertheless, whenever you desire, you may slaughter and eat meat, according to the blessing which the Lord your God has granted you in any of your cities; the ritually clean and unclean alike may eat it, as if it were a gazelle or deer. 16. Only the blood you may not eat; you should pour it out on the ground like water. 17. You are not permitted to eat in your cities the tithe of your grain and of your wine, as well as of your oil, of your herds and of your flocks, and of all your votive offerings, which you will vow, and your freewill offerings, as well as your personal

Apparatus, Chapter 12

[a] So also Y, whereas Sperber's main text has: "abandon," as does the Hebrew.

[b] l has the plural.

[c] v, b, g, and l add: "the tithe of," while D adds it in the plural.

[d] D has: "to expel."

[e] M has: "expel."

[f] j omits, as do the LXX, the Vg., and Vetus Latina.

contributions. 18. Rather, you should eat it before the Lord your God, in the place that the Lord your God will choose; you and your son and your daughter, as well as your servant and your maid and the Levite of your *city;*[7] and you should rejoice before the Lord your God in all your undertakings. 19. Watch yourself, lest you *keep away*[a] the *Levite*[b] as long as you live on your land. 20. When the Lord your God will enlarge your territory as He has *promised you,*[8] and you will say, 'I am going to eat meat, because your body has the craving to eat meat, you may eat meat as much as your body craves.' 21. Moreover, if the place that the Lord your God will choose to let His *Shekhinah*[2] dwell there, is too far from you, then you may slaughter any of your cattle or your sheep which the Lord has given you, as I commanded you, and you may eat in your city as much as your body craves. 22. However, you should eat it as the gazelle and deer are eaten, the ritually unclean and clean alike may eat it. 23. Only, control yourself not to eat the blood, for the blood is the life, and you may not eat the life with the flesh. 24. Do not eat it, but pour it out on the ground like water. 25. Do not eat it, so that you may fare well and your descendants after you; for you will be doing what is proper before the Lord. 26. *Only*[c] your consecrated offerings and your votive offerings that you may have, take, and bring to the place that the Lord will choose. 27. Then you should present your burnt offerings, the flesh together with the blood, on the altar of the Lord your God, whereas the blood of your *sanctified sacrifices*[4] should be poured out on the altar of the Lord your God, while the flesh you may eat. 28. Be careful to obey all these matters which I command you, in order that you and your descendents after you may fare well forever; for you should be doing what is right and proper before the Lord your God. 29. When the Lord your God will destroy before you the nations whom you are about to invade and *inherit,*[d] and you have *inherited*[e] them and settled in their land, 30. watch yourself lest you will become ensnared *in their ways*[9] after they have been destroyed before you; lest you inquire about their *idols,*[10] saying, 'How do these nations worship their *idols?*[10] I, too, will do likewise.' 31. Do not act this way *before*[1] the Lord your God, for they have engaged in practices towards their idols with every abominable act that the Lord detests, for they *even*[f] burned their sons and their daughters in fire for their *idols.*[10]

Notes, Chapter 12

[1]See Gen. Chap. 4, n. 1.
[2]See Introduction VII D.3.
[3]Lit. "come."
[4]See Exod. Chap. 10, n. 11.
[5]Lit. "everything that is proper in his eyes."
[6]Lit. "and the."
[7]See Gen. Chap. 22, n. 13.
[8]Lit. "spoken to you."
[9]Lit. "after them."
[10]See Introduction VII A.3.

CHAPTER 13

1. You should diligently follow *everything*[a] that I command you; do not add to it nor take away from it. 2. If there appears among you a prophet or a dream diviner, and he gives you a sign or a portent, 3. and the sign or the portent of which he has spoken to you, saying, 'Let us follow *the idols of the nations*[1] whom you have not *experienced*[2] and let us worship them,' takes place, 4. do not accept the words of that prophet or *of*[b] that dream diviner, for the Lord your God is testing you, to find out whether you love the Lord your God with your whole heart and with your whole soul. 5. *Follow the worship*[c] *of*[3] the Lord your God and revere Him; observe His commandments and *accept His Memra;*[4] worship *before*[5] Him and *stay close to His reverence.*[6] 6. As for that prophet or dream diviner, he shall be put to death, for he uttered rebellion against the Lord your God—who brought you out of the land of Egypt and who redeemed you from the place of slavery—to make you stray from the path that the Lord your God commanded you to follow; so you must remove *the evil doer*[7] from your midst. 7. If your brother—your {own} mother's son, or your son, or your daughter, or *the wife of your covenant,*[8] or *your closest friend*[9] secretly entices you, saying, 'Let us go and worship *the idols of the nations,*[1] whom you and your ancestors have not *experienced,*[2] 8. from among *the idols of the nations*[1] around you, who are near to you or far away from you, from one end of the earth to the other (end of the earth).' 9. Do not consent to him nor *accept*[10] *from him,*[d] and do not have compassion for him, nor show affection for him or show mercy towards him. 10. Rather you must surely put him to death; your hand must be the first in putting him to death, and the hand of the rest of the people thereafter. 11. In fact stone him to death, for he sought to make you stray from *the reverence of*[11] the Lord your God, who brought you out of the land of Egypt, from the place of slavery. 12. Now all of Israel will hear and be afraid, and they will no longer commit such an evil act in your midst. 13. If you hear it said in one of your cities, that the Lord your God is giving you to dwell in, 14. that some wicked men from among you have gone out and have led the inhabitants of their city astray, saying 'Let us go and worship *the idols of the nations*[1] whom you have not *experienced,*[2]' 15. then you must investigate and inquire and interrogate thoroughly; and if this matter proves to be true, this abominable act has been committed among you, 16. you must utterly destroy the inhabitants of that city by <putting it to> the sword, annihilate it and all that is in it, as well as its cattle by <putting it to> the sword. 17. Now as for all of the plunder, you should gather it into the *open square,*[12] and totally burn the city and all of its plunder in fire before the Lord your God; it should remain an everlasting heap of ruin, never to be rebuilt. 18. Let nothing of the condemned material cling to your hand, so that the Lord

Apparatus, Chapter 13

[a] D has: "every commandment."
[b] D, g, and b have: "to," as does the Hebrew.
[c] D and c have: "reverence."
[d] G has: "his word."

may recoil from His powerful anger and render you compassion, and in His compassion make you more numerous as He promised your ancestors on oath. 19. For you will be *accepting the Memra of*[4] the Lord your God to observe all His commandments which I command you this day, to do what is proper before the Lord your God.

Notes, Chapter 13

[1]See Introduction VII A.3 and ns. 10, 11, 12.

[2]Lit. "known."

[3]See Num. Chap. 14, n. 32.

[4]See Gen. Chap. 22, n. 14.

[5]See Gen. Chap. 4, n. 1.

[6]See above Chap. 10, n. 10.

[7]The Hebrew has: "the evil" which the Targum interprets to mean that evil is removed by removing the force behind it—"the evil doer." Tgs. Ps.-Jon. and Neof. are similar but pluralize the substantive.

[8]The Hebrew has: *hêqéḵā* "your bosom," which the Pal. Tgs. paraphrase slightly—Ps.-Jon. "who sleeps in your bosom," as against the Frg. Tg. (V) "who sleeps with you." Tg. Onq. however renders *qĕyāmāk* concerning which the various commentaries differ as to its meaning. Schefftel (*Bi'ure Onqelos.* Munich, 1888, p. 242) points out that *qĕyām* in the Targum is a euphemism for "bosom" of the Hebrew. In that vein, he cites Exod. 21:8 where the Hebrew "who *betrothed* her to himself" is rendered by the verb *qym* in the Targum as is the case in *ibid.* 22:15, where "he should surely *endow her to be his wife*" is rendered by *qymh yqymynh.* S.A. Wertheimer (*Or Ha-Targum.* Jerusalem, 1935, p. 93f.) conjectures that *qym* means "thigh," citing a Jerusalem Targum to Gen. 24:9, which he says exists only in the Arukh, but which likewise exists in the Frg. Tg. (V) to Gen. 24:2. Löwenstein (*Nefesh Ha-Ger, op. cit.,* p. 26) takes *qym* to mean "covenant," its literal translation, the meaning being "the wife of your covenant," i.e., the one who adheres to the same covenant as you do. Y. Koraḥ (*Marpe Lashon, op. cit.,* on this verse) likewise renders *qymk* here according to its literal meaning "your covenant" citing Mal. 2:14 where the phrase "wife of your covenant" actually occurs in the Hebrew and is there rendered by the Tg. Neb. the same way as in Tg. Onq. here. Koraḥ theorizes that the reason the Targum deviates here is because he considered the association of marriage (here expressed by the term "wife of") with bosom to be an improper one, as bosom is usually associated with the act of lying as in 2 Sam. 12:3; 1 Kgs. 3:20. He then suggests that the use of "covenant" here is only to be understood in a figurative sense as the common Arabic expression which is made by a strong person to a weak one when promising to protect him—"come into my bosom," meaning that he should trust his covenant with him in that he would not lie to him.

It appears, however, that the Targum rendered Hebrew *ḥyq* here as *qym* simply because he read it *ḥwq* instead, which is extensively rendered *qym* (cf. Exod. 15:25; Lev. 3:17; Num. 15:15; 18:23; and Deut. 4:45, especially Gen. 9:16; Exod. 30:21; and Exod. 12:14 where Hebrew *brît 'ôlam, ḥōq 'ôlām,* and *ḥuqqat 'ôlām* interchange). Furthermore, retaining its literal meaning "covenant" is very relevant here, as the verse deals with seduction into idolatry which involves betraying the covenant of God. Thus, the translation in the Targum is indeed interpretive, meaning, "the wife of your covenant," whom you trust, as she believes in the same covenant as you do. The Syr. is the only ancient translation which is here identical to the Targum. Cf. also Deut. 28:54, 56 and Mic. 7:5 where the Targum (Onqelos in the former, and Jonathan in the latter passage) renders Hebrew *ḥyq* as *qym,* as well.

[9]Lit. "your friend who is as <close to you as> your soul."

[10]See Gen. Chap. 16, n. 1.

[11]See Introduction VII B.3.

[12]The Hebrew *rĕḥôb* is here rendered interpretively to mean "the open square" or "public square" of the city, where the ceremony of burning everything and everybody involved in idolatry was made a public spectacle. In contrast, in Gen. 19:2 where the term simply means "street," involving no public spectacle, it is rendered literally in the Targum by the identical root in Aramaic. Tgs. Ps.-Jon. and Neof. have *plṭy'* "open place" <Greek πλατεῖα, and the Syr. *šṭḥ* with the same meaning.

CHAPTER 14

1. You are children *before*[1] the Lord your God; do not gash yourselves or make a bald spot between your eyes because of the dead. 2. For you are a consecrated people *before*[1] the Lord your God, and you the Lord chose to be His *beloved*[2] nation, from all other nations on the face of the earth. 3. Do not eat anything that is abominable. 4. This is the <type of> animal you may eat: *Oxen,*[3] *lambs*[3] from ewes and *kids*[4] from he-goats, 5. the deer, the gazelle, the roebuck, the wild goat, the ibex, the *wild ox,*[5] and the mountain sheep. 6. Every animal whose claw is split and has two split hoofs, as well as bringing up the cud among animals, it you may eat. 7. But this <type> you may not eat—of those who bring up the cud or have true split claws: The camel, and the rabbit, as well as the rockbadger, for they bring up the cud, but their claw is not split; they are ritually unclean for you, 8. and the pig, though it has a split claw but does not chew the cud, is unclean for you; you should not eat of their flesh, nor should you touch their carcasses. 9. This <type> you may eat of all that is in the water—whatever has fins and scales; 10. and whatever does not have fins and scales, you may not eat; it is unclean for you. 11. You may eat every clean bird. 12. But of the following you may not eat: The eagle, the sea eagle, and the black eagle, 13. and the red kite and black vulture, as well as the vulture according to its kind, 14. and every type of raven according to its kind, 15. and the ostrich, as well as the night hawk, and the sea gull, as well as <every> kind of hawk; 16. and the little owl, as well as the big owl, and the white owl; 17. and the pelican, as well as the gier eagle, and the cormorant, 18. and the stork as well as the kite according to its kind, and the woodcock and the bat. 19. Now all swarming creatures among the fowl are unclean for you. 20. You may eat any clean winged creature. 21. You may not eat any carcass, give it to the *uncircumcised transient*[6] who is in your *city*[7] and let him eat it, or sell it to a foreigner; for you are a people consecrated *before*[1] the Lord your God; *do not consume meat with milk.*[8] 22. You should set aside a tenth part of all the produce of your sowing, which the field yields every year. 23. Now you may consume the tithes of your grain, (your) wine, and (your) oil, as well as the firstborn of your herds and your flocks before the Lord your God, in the place where He will choose to rest His *Shekhinah,*[9] so that you may learn to be in reverence *before*[1] the Lord your God forever. 24. But if the journey is too much for you, because the place where the Lord your God has chosen to rest His *Shekhinah*[9] is too far for you, and because the Lord your God has blessed you, 25. *you should covert them*[10] into money and wrap up the money, then go to the place that the Lord your God will choose. 26. There *spend*[11] the money on anything you choose—cattle, sheep, wine, new or old, or anything you may desire; and you shall eat there before the Lord your God and rejoice—you, and your household. 27. But as for the Levite of your city, do not *abandon*[a] him, for he has no inherited portion among you. 28. At the end of <every> three years, you should bring out the full tithe of your yield of that year and store it in your *cities.*[7] 29. Then the

Apparatus, Chapter 14

[a] i has: "keep away." See above Chap. 12, Apparatus, note *a*.

Levite, because he has no inherited portion among you, and the alien, as well as the orphan and widow, should come and eat to their satisfaction, so that the Lord your God may bless you in all your endeavors that you undertake.

CHAPTER 15

1. At the end of <every> seven years you should practice remission of debts. 2. Now this should be the nature of the remission, in that *every man who is a creditor,*[1] who claims a debt from his fellowman, should not seek <payment> from his fellowman or from his kinsmen, for a remission of debt has been proclaimed *before*[2] the Lord. 3. From a *foreigner*[3] you may seek <payment> but that what is due to you from your

Notes, Chapter 14

[1]See Gen. Chap. 4, n. 1.
[2]See Exod. Chap. 19, n. 5.
[3]See Gen. Chap. 21, n. 7.
[4]The Hebrew has *śeh* "lamb," which is here rendered by *gdî* "kid." This identification of *śeh* with *gdî* is reflected in the following Midrash—Gen. Rab. LXX:7, p. 803f: "A heathen asked Rabbi Meir saying to him: With what do you redeem the firstling of your donkey? He said to him: With a lamb, as it is written (Exod. 34:20) 'But the firstling of a donkey you should redeem with a lamb.' Said he to him: What if he has no lamb? So he said to him: Then with a goat. Said he to him: How do you know this? He said: Because it is written 'you should take it from the sheep or from the goats' (Exod. 12:5). Said he to him: Those are for the Paschal lamb. He then said to him: *gdî* is also called *śeh.* Said he to him: How do you know that? So he said to him: Because it is written (Deut. 14:5) 'This is the <type of> animal you may eat: The *śeh* of lambs and the *śeh* of goats.' He thereupon proceeded to kiss him on his head."
[5]The Hebrew *tĕ'ô* here rendered "wild ox" (*tôrbālā*) by the Targum is likewise considered by the Rabbis (cf. m. Kil. VIII:6) who consider this animal as "cattle" in opposition to R. Jose's view according to which it is a "beast." The identical argument is cited in the Talmud where the Rabbis, in fact, cite the Targum here as support for their contention, for which cf. b. Ḥul. 80a and y. Kil VIII:6, p. 31c. Cf. further Berliner, *Targum Onkelos: Einleitung zum Targum Onkelos.* Berlin, 1884, p. 241, n. 1.
[6]See Lev. Chap. 25, n. 10.
[7]See Gen. Chap. 22, n. 13.
[8]See Exod. Chap. 23, n. 18.
[9]See Introduction VII D.3.
[10]Lit. "you should give."

Notes, Chapter 15

[1]The Hebrew has lit. "every possessor of a loan of his hand," which the Targum renders "every man <who is> the possessor of a debt," i.e., creditor, omitting to translate the figurative "of his hand." Tg. Ps.-Jon. likewise has "every person <who is> possessor of a loan," while Tg. Neof. translates "everyman who is possessor of a debt" making "his hand" the accusative of the preceding verb "release," and where "hand" is to be understood as "claim"—thus every man who is the possessor of a debt, should release his claim from it. The Syr. is similar to Tg. Neof. but, like Tg. Onq., omits translating "his hand."
[2]See Gen. Chap. 4, n. 1.
[3]See Gen. Chap. 17, n. 7.

kinsman, you must remit. 4. Nevertheless, there should be no poor among you, for the Lord will surely bless you in the land that the Lord your God is giving you as an inherited possession. 5. If only you will thoroughly *accept the Memra of*[4] the Lord your God, to diligently observe this entire precept, which I order you this day. 6. For the Lord your God will bless you as He has *promised you,*[5] in that you will extend loans to many nations, but you will not <need to> make a loan; you will dominate many nations, but they will not dominate you. 7. If there should be a poor person among your kinsmen in one of your *cities*[6] of *your*[a] land, that the Lord your God is giving you, do not harden your heart, nor *tightfist*[b] your hand towards your poor kinsmen. 8. Rather you must completely open your hand to him, and graciously lend him sufficiently for whatever he needs. 9. Be careful lest you harbor the evil thought in your heart which says: *The seventh year,*[c] the year of remission, is approaching; so that *you will look unfavorably*[7] at your poor kinsmen, and give him nothing; for then he will cry out *before*[2] the Lord, and you will incur guilt. 10. Rather give him graciously and do not *feel bad*[8] while giving him, for on account of this matter the Lord your God will bless you in all your efforts and in all your undertakings. 11. For there will never cease to be a poor person within the land; therefore I command you as follows: You must completely open your hand to your kinsmen and to your poor in your land. 12. If your kinsman, an *Israelite*[9] man or *Israelite*[9] woman is sold to you, he should serve you six years, and in the seventh year you should release him from you, as a free person. 13. When you release him from you as a free person, do not release him empty-handed. 14. <Rather> liberally set aside for him from your flock and from your threshing floor, as well as from your winepress, with which the Lord your God has blessed you, <and> give <it> to him. 15. Now you should remember that you were a slave in the land of Egypt, and the Lord your God redeemed you; therefore, I issue you this command this day. 16. But if he should say to you: 'I do not want to depart from you'; because he loves you and your household, since he is well off with you, 17. then take an awl and put it through his ear into the door, and he will become a *laboring slave*[10] to you forever; do likewise with your female slave. 18. Do not *feel aggrieved*[11] when you do release him from you, for his six years of labor to you have been worth twice the fee for a hired hand; moreover, the Lord your God will bless you in all you will do. 19. You should consecrate *before*[2] the Lord your God every male firstborn that is born among your herd and among your flock; do not work with the firstborn of your oxen, nor shear the firstborn of your sheep. 20. You should eat them every year before the Lord your God, in the place which the Lord will choose—you and *the members of*[12] your house. 21. Now if it has a defect, lameness or blindness, *any serious defect,*[d] do not sacrifice it *before*[2] the Lord your God. 22. You should eat it in

Apparatus, Chapter 15

[a] h has: "the," as do the LXX, the Syr., the Vg., and the Sam. Heb.
[b] D has: "contract," or "fold."
[c] A and v have: "the year of the Sabbatical."
[d] M has: "anything serious."

Apparatus, Chapter 16

[a] D omits; the Hebrew does not have it.
[b] D omits; the Hebrew does not have it.
[c] j and l add: "your God," as do 2 Hebrew mss., the Sam. Heb., the Syr., and the Vg. as well as some miniscule LXX codices.

your *city,*[6] the unclean as well as the clean, as if it were the meat of the gazelle or the deer. 23. Only do not consume its blood, <rather> pour it out on the ground like water.

CHAPTER 16

1. Observe the month of Abib and celebrate the Passover before the Lord your God, for in the month of Abib the Lord your God brought you out of Egypt *and performed miracles for you*[a] *at*[1] night. 2. You should sacrifice as the Passover before the Lord your God <an animal> *from the young*[b] *sheep, and as the sanctified sacrifice*[2] *from the cattle,*[2] at the place where the *Lord*[c] will choose to rest His *Shekhinah.*[3] 3. Do not eat anything leavened with it; {for} seven days you should eat with it unleavened bread, the bread of affliction, since you departed from the land of Egypt in haste; in order that you will remember the day of your departure from the land of Egypt all the days of your life. 4. Let no yeast be seen throughout your territory {for} seven days, nor should any of the flesh of what you slaughtered on the evening of the first day, remain overnight until morning. 5. You are not permitted to slaughter the Passover sacrifice in any of the *cities*[4] that the Lord your God is giving you. 6. Except at the place that the Lord your God will

Notes, Chapter 15 (Cont.)

[4]See Gen. Chap. 22, n. 14.
[5]Lit. "spoke to you."
[6]See Gen. Chap. 22, n. 13.
[7]Lit. "your eyes will feel badly."
[8]Lit. "your heart should not feel bad."
[9]See Exod. Chap. 21, n. 2.
[10]See Exod. Chap. 21, n. 5.
[11]Lit. "let it feel difficult in your eyes."
[12]See Gen. Chap. 7, n. 1.

Notes, Chapter 16

[1]This addition in the Targum, which interrupts the sequence—"the Lord your God brought you out of Egypt at night," is reflected in the following brief discussion of this passage in Sifre (*Rĕʾēh* CXXVIII, p. 186): "'God brought you out of Egypt <at> night.' Did they actually depart at night? But they really departed during the day, as it says: 'On the day following the Passover . . .' (Num. 33:3). Rather it teaches that they were *redeemed* at night." The Targum addition "and performed miracles for you" refers to the "redemption" stated in this Midrash.

[2]The Hebrew has simply—"sheep and cattle" which the Sifre (*ibid.* CXXIX, p. 187) questions as follows: "Does not the Passover sacrifice come strictly from lambs or goats (according to Exod. 12:5)? If so, why does it say 'sheep and cattle' (Deut. 16:2)? (Rather) the sheep was for the Passover sacrifice, the cattle for the Festive Offering (*ḥăgîgāh*)." Cf. further Mekhilta *Bōʾ* IV, where Rabbi Aqiba and three other Tannaim offer the same interpretation, whereas Rabbi offers a different explanation, also found in m. Šeqal. II:5 and here supported by Ps.-Jon.

[3]See Introduction VII D.3.

[4]See Gen. Chap. 22, n. 13.

choose to rest His *Shekhinah,*[3] there you should slaughter the Passover sacrifice in the evening at sunset, the very time you departed from Egypt. 7. Now you should cook, and you should eat at the place which the Lord your God chooses, then in the morning turn and go <back> to your *city.*[d] 8. Six days you should eat unleavened bread, then on the seventh day hold an assembly[e] before the Lord your God; you shall do no work. 9. Count off seven weeks, from the time when the sickle is first <put> to the harvest of the sheaf *for the wave offering,*[5] you should count off seven weeks. 10. Then you should observe the Festival of Weeks before the Lord your God by giving a freewill offering in proportion to how much the Lord your God has blessed you. 11. Now you should rejoice before the Lord your God, you and your son and your daughter, as well as your servant and your maid, and the Levite of your *city,*[4] as well as the alien, (and) the orphan and the widow who are among you, at the place that the Lord your God will choose to rest His *Shekhinah.*[3] 12. Moreover, you should remember that you were a slave in Egypt, and <therefore> diligently observe these decrees. 13. Observe the Feast of Booths {for} seven days after the ingathering from your threshing floor and your winepress. 14. Now you should rejoice in your festival, you and your son and your daughter, as well as your maid and your servant, as well as the Levite, and the alien, (and) the orphan and widow, who are in your *city.*[4] 15. You should celebrate before the Lord your God {for} seven days, at the place that the Lord your God will choose; for the Lord your God will bless you in all your harvest and in all your undertakings, and you will only be happy. 16. Three times a year all your males should appear before the Lord your God, at the place which He will choose: On the Festival of Unleavened Bread and on the Festival of Weeks, as well as on the Festival of Booths; *but they should not appear*[6] empty-handed before the Lord; 17. each man with a gift he can afford, according to the blessing which the Lord your God has bestowed upon you. 18. You should appoint judges and law-enforcers for each tribe, in all your *cities,*[4] which the Lord your God is giving you; and they should judge the people with true justice. 19. You shall not pervert justice, you shall not show favoritism, nor shall you *accept*[7] a bribe, for a bribe blinds the eyes of the wise and corrupts the words of the upright. 20. You should pursue the truth in every form, so that you may live, and take possession of the land that the Lord your God is giving you. 21. Do not plant any tree dedicated to Asherah beside the altar of the Lord your God that you made. 22. Moreover, do not set up a statue, which the Lord your God *abhors.*[f]

Apparatus, Chapter 16 (Cont.)

[d] J, G, and M have: "tent," as does the Hebrew.

[e] h and l have the plural, while the Sam. Heb. has: "festival."

[f] h has the literal: "hates."

Apparatus, Chapter 17

[a] J, D, y_b, d_2, and Rashi have: "your city," while l has the literal: "your gate." Tg. Ps.-Jon. is identical to Vat. 448, while Tg. Neof. reads: "your cities."

[b] l has: "concealed from."

[c] k has: "and to the," as does the Syr. and Tg. Neof.

CHAPTER 17

1. Do not sacrifice before the Lord your God an ox or a sheep that has any type of serious defect; for that is abhorrent before the Lord your God. 2. If there is found among you in one of the *cities*[1] that the Lord your God is giving you, a man or a woman who does what is evil *before*[2] the Lord your God, in violation of His covenant, 3. by going and worshiping *the idols of the nations*[3] and bowing down to them, or to the sun, or to the moon, or to the heavenly host, something I never commanded, 4. and you have been informed or have heard {of it}' then you should thoroughly investigate {it}' and if indeed the situation is confirmed to be true—this abominable act was committed in Israel, 5. you should bring out that man or that woman, who committed this evil act, to *the entrance of your court*[a1]—that very man and woman—and stone them to death. 6. *The one condemned to execution*[4] should be put to death on the word of two or three witnesses; he should not be put to death on the word of one witness. 7. The hands of the witnesses should be the first against him to put him to death and thereafter the hands of all the people; and so you must remove the *evildoer*[5] from your midst. 8. If a case is *too far out for*[b] you to decide in judgment, be it *homicide or civil law, or {even} involving the leprosy plague,*[6] matters of dispute in your city,[1] then you should proceed to go up to the place that the Lord your God will choose. 9. When you will come to the priests *who are*[c] Levites, and to the judge presiding at that time and make an inquiry, they will relate to

Notes, Chapter 16 (Cont.)

[5]This addition in the Targum, which defines the sheaf as that designated for the wave offering, is based on Lev. 23:10, 11, 15, 16, where the command is given to bring the first sheaf of the harvest on the day after the Sabbath to the priest for a wave offering, whereupon the counting of the seven weeks begins. Tg. Neof. also has this addition (using *'npwth* in contrast to Tg. Onq.'s *'rmwt'*).

[6]The Hebrew *wĕlo yērā'eh ('et pnê...)* is grammatically difficult—the verb being in the *niphal* followed by the accusative particle *'et*. The Targum resolves the difficulty by rendering *yērā'eh* into the *ithpe'el* of *ḥzy*—"to see," pluralizing it, and translating *'et* by *qdm*. This retains the passive character of the verb which is here followed by the logical preposition in the form of *qdm*—"before." Likewise, Tgs. Neof. and Ps.-Jon. which have: "you are not permitted to appear before the Lord your God empty-handed of any precepts." The Syr. too has *qdm* for Hebrew *'et* here, but keeps the verb in the *ithpe'el* singular, thus—"you may not appear before the Lord your God empty-handed."

[7]See Gen. Chap. 4, n. 8.

Notes, Chapter 17

[1]See below Chap. 21, n. 13.

[2]See Gen. Chap. 4, n. 1.

[3]See Introduction VII A.3.

[4]The Hebrew *hammēt* must here be understood to mean the doomed person, hence the interpretive translation of the Targum—"the one condemned to execution"; likewise Tgs. Neof., Ps.-Jon. and the Syr. "the one condemned to death."

[5]See above Chap. 13, n. 7.

[6]Lit. "between blood and blood, between law and law, as well as between plague and plague." The last of these is rendered in the Targum in a more defined form "leprosy plague," an interpretation which is in agreement with Rabbinic opinion, as reflected in the following sources: y. Sanh. IX:4, p. 30a "Between plague and plague' (Deut. 17:8) between a locked-up leper and a confirmed leper. 'Between plague and plague' embracing leprosy in man, houses and garments." The latter part of this Talmudic passage also exists in b. Sanh. 87a; b. Nid. 19a; and the Midrash Sifre *Šôp̱ṭîm* CLII, p. 205.

you the *verdict*[7] in the case. 10. Then act on the basis of the *verdict*[7] that they relate to you from that place which the Lord will choose, and diligently follow according to all that they will instruct you. 11. You should act on the basis of the word of the Law that they will teach you, and on the basis of the decision that they will tell you; do not deviate from the *verdict*[7] that they will relate to you, either to the right or to the left. 12. Now the man who will act presumptuously by not obeying the priest, who stands ministering there *before*[2] the Lord, or the judge, that man *should be executed*[8] and so you must remove the *evildoer*[5] from Israel. 13. Whereupon all the people will hear and be afraid, and will not act presumptuously again. 14. When you will enter the land that the Lord your God is giving you, and you will take possession of it and settle in it, you will say: 'I would like to set a king over me like all the nations around me.' 15. You may certainly set a king over yourself, one whom the Lord your God will choose; you should set over yourself a king from among your kinsmen; you are not permitted to set over yourself a foreigner, one who is not your kinsman. 16. Only he must not own too many horses, nor could he send the people back to Egypt to acquire more horses *for himself,*[9] since the Lord has told you: 'Do not ever return that way again!' 17. Neither should he own too many wives, so that his heart will not lead <him> astray, nor should he own too much silver and gold. 18. Now when he is seated on his royal throne, he should inscribe for himself a copy of this law on a scroll, from that which is before the priests, who are Levites. 19. Moreover, it should be with him, and he should read it all the days of his life, so that he will learn to be in reverence *before*[2] the Lord his God, to diligently observe all the words of this law and these decrees; 20. so that he will not act haughtily towards his fellowmen, nor deviate from the precept to the right or to the left; so that he may prolong the days of his reign—he and his descendants—in the midst of Israel.

CHAPTER 18

1. The priests who are Levites, in fact the entire tribe of Levi, shall have no portion or inherited possession with Israel; they shall live off the Lord's offering, that is their inheritance. 2. Now he should have no inheritance among his brothers; his inheritance *consists of the gifts which the Lord assigned to him,*[1] as He *promised*[2] him. 3. This then should *be*[a] what is due to the priests from the people, from those who offer sacrifices, whether an ox or a sheep, he must give the shoulder, the *cheek,*[3] and the stomach to the priest. 4. You should *give*[b] him the firstfruits of your grain, your wine, and your oil, as well as the first shearing of your sheep. 5. For the Lord your God chose him from all

Apparatus, Chapter 18

[a] b and d_2 add: "the law," which results in a double translation for Hebrew *mišpaṭ*—"the law," and "what is due."

[b] g and l have: "set aside for."

[c] Y and T have: "serve."

[d] G has: "the abhorrent of the Lord," while c adds: "your God," as do some Hebrew mss., the Sam. Heb., the LXX, and the Syr.

your tribes to be in attendance for service in the name of the Lord forever, he and his descendants. 6. Now if the Levite comes from any of your *cities*[4] throughout Israel where he resides, if he were to come with his entire determination to the place that the Lord will choose, 7. he may serve in the name of the Lord his God, like all his fellow Levites, who *stand in service*[c] there before the Lord. 8. They shall *receive*[5] equal shares of the dues, besides *the watch of that same week, for thus have the ancestors established.*[6] 9. When you enter the land that the Lord your God is giving you, do not learn to imitate the abominable practices of these nations. 10. Let no one be found among you, one who leads his son or his daughter through the fire, one who practices divination, sorcery, interprets omens, engages in witchcraft, 11. or one who casts spells, or one who consults a medium or necromancer, or one who inquires of the dead. 12. For all those who engage in these {practices} are *abhorrent before the Lord,*[d] and because of these abominations, the Lord your God expels them before you. 13. Be complete *in your reverence of*[7] the Lord your God. 14. For these nations whom you are

Notes, Chapter 17 (Cont.)

[7]Lit. "word," or "matter."

[8]The Hebrew has: "should die" which is interpretively rendered to mean he "should be executed" (by strangulation according to m. Sanh. XI:2 and b. Sanh. 86b). Similarly, Tgs. Ps.-Jon. and Neof., the Syr., and the Sam. Tg. (J).

[9]An insertion, also in Tg. Neof., the Syr., the Vg. and LXX, but implied in the Hebrew.

Notes, Chapter 18

[1]See Num. Chap. 18, n. 10.

[2]Lit. "spoke (to)."

[3]The Hebrew has the plural which the Targum here renders into the singular, an interpretive translation also reflected in the following Sifre (*Šopṭîm* CLXV, p. 215) "'and the cheeks' (Deut. 18:3)—this refers to the lower cheek." The LXX, Tg. Ps.-Jon., the Sam. Tg., and Tg. Neof. have the plural while the Syr., like Tg. Onq., has the singular here.

[4]See Gen. Chap. 22, n. 13.

[5]Lit. "eat."

[6]The Hebrew has: "besides <the benefits he received> from the sale of his ancestral possessions." The Rabbis in the Talmud (b. Suk. 56a) and Midrash (Sifre *ibid.*, CLXIX, p. 217) ask: "What did the ancestors sell to each other? (They made as it were an agreement of sale saying: 'I take [the ordinary priestly dues during] my week and you take [them during] your week" [according to b. Suk. 56a, whereas in the Sifre passage the order is reversed].) This agreement took place, according to Rashi, during the days of David and Samuel when the system of rotations—the so-called *mišmārôt* were established (as stated in 1 Chr 9:22, 23). These were the *mišmārôt* <*šmr* ("keep, watch")—each one of which consisted of a guard of priests and Levites, of one of the divisions that carried on the Temple services in rotation. Each *mišmār* in turn was subdivided into smaller groups each being designated a *bêt 'ab*—"family." It is this *bêt 'ab* precisely to which the term *'ăbāhātā'* (here rendered "ancestors") in the Targum refers. According to an elaborate discussion in the Talmud (b. Ta'an. 27a), these *mišmarôt* numbered eight originally and were instituted by Moses for Israel (four from the family of Eleazar and four from the family of Ithamar—the two sons of Aaron). David and Samuel came along and eventually increased them to twenty-four. The Tg. Ps.-Jon.—"besides the surplus of the sacrifices which the priests eat that Eleazar and Ithamar their ancestors made them inherit"—here reflects the discussion in the above-mentioned Talmudic passage. The Frg. Tg. (V) and the Tg. Neof. m. are closer to the earlier cited Sifre in rendering—"besides the purchases which they sold him according to the ancestors," i.e., "besides the right acquired by transactions between his ancestors." Tg. Neof., on the other hand, has: "besides the surplus of his sacrifices, which their ancestors gave them as an inheritance."

[7]See Introduction VII B.3.

dispossessing listen to sorcerers and diviners, but as for you, the Lord your God has not assigned these to you. 15. {Rather} the Lord your God will raise up for you a prophet like me, from among your own brothers; *him you should obey.*[8] 16. Exactly as you have requested *from*[e] before the Lord your God at Ḥoreb on the day of the assembly, saying, 'I do not wish to continue hearing the voice of *the Memra of*[9] the Lord my God, nor do I wish to ever again see this great fire, lest I die.' 17. Whereupon the Lord said to me, 'They have spoken to the point.' 18. I will raise up a prophet for them from among their own people, like yourself; then I will put the words of My prophecy in his mouth, and he will speak to them all that I commanded him. 19. Now the man who will not *obey*[8] My words, which he will speak in My name, *My Memra*[f] will seek him out. 20. But the prophet who presumes to speak an oracle in My name, which I did not command him to utter or who speaks in the name of *the idols of the nations,*[10] that prophet *should be executed.*[11] 21. Now if you say to yourself, 'How would I discern the oracle that the Lord did not utter?' 22. If the prophet speaks in the name of the Lord, and the oracle does not take place or come true, that is an oracle that the Lord has not uttered, the prophet has uttered it presumptuously; do not be afraid of him.

CHAPTER 19

1. When the Lord your God will have destroyed the nations whose land the Lord your God is giving you, you will have dispossessed them and settled in their cities and in their houses, 2. you should set aside three cities in the land that the Lord your God is giving you to possess. 3. You should prepare the road <to them> and divide into three parts the territory of the land that the Lord your God has given you as an inherited possession, where a manslayer may have a place to flee to. 4. Now this is the case of the manslayer who may flee there *and*[a] survive, one who had killed his fellowman without forethought, and without *previously*[1] having had enmity towards him, 5. as for instance, if one goes with his fellowman into the woods to cut wood, and as his hand *weakened*[b] <in grasping the handle> while he was cutting the wood, the ax-head slipped off the wooden handle and *struck*[2] his fellowman so that he dies; he should flee to one of these cities and survive. 6. Otherwise, the blood avenger might pursue the manslayer because *of his rage,*[3] and he might overtake him if the distance is <too> great; then he might kill him even though he does not have *the guilt of a judgment for murder,*[4] since he had no

Apparatus, Chapter 18 (Cont.)

[e] l omits.

[f] c has: "I," as does the Hebrew.

Apparatus, Chapter 19

[a] k has: "in order to."

[b] M, v, b, *d, g, and Rashi have: "vacillated."

[c] Lit. "and he should die," whereas h and l have: "to be executed," lit. "and he should be executed," as do Tg. Ps.-Jon., the Syr., and the Sam. Heb., but Tg. Neof. has: "and he should kill him." See further on this, Chap. 18, n. 1 above.

[d] l adds: "and the Levites."

enmity towards him *previously.*[1] 7. I, therefore, command you as follows: Set aside three cities. 8. When the Lord your God will enlarge your territory as He swore to your ancestors, and He will give you all the land that He *promised*[5] to give to your ancestors, 9. if you will diligently observe this entire precept which I issue you this day—to love the Lord your God and always *follow the paths that are proper before Him,*[6] then you should add three more cities to these three. 10. So that the blood of the innocent will not be spilled within your land, that the Lord your God is giving you as an inherited possession, that you may not have *the guilt of a judgment for murder*[7] on you. 11. If, however, a man hates his fellowman and lies in wait for him, then assaults him and kills him, he then flees to one of these cities, 12. the elders of his city should send <for him> and bring him back from there, then hand him over to the blood avenger *to die.*[c] 13. Do not have compassion for him; you should remove from Israel *those who shed*[7] innocent blood, that you fare well. 14. Do not alter your neighbor's boundary stone that was set up by *your*[8] predecessors, in your inherited portion that you will possess, in the land that the Lord your God is giving you as an inheritance. 15. A single witness may not rise up <to testify> against any person for wrongs or transgressions, or for any offense he may have committed; a matter can only be confirmed on the word of two witnesses, or on the word of three witnesses. 16. If a *false*[9] witness should rise up against a person to testify maliciously against him, 17. the two men who have the dispute should then stand before the Lord, before the *priests*[d] and the judges who are <in authority> at that time. 18. Now the judges should make a thorough investigation, and if the man who testified

Notes, Chapter 18 (Cont.)

[8]Lit. "from him you should accept," for which see Gen. Chap. 16, n. 1. Similarly, in vs. 19 below—lit. "accept."

[9]See Introduction VII D.1.

[10]See Introduction VII A.3.

[11]The Hebrew has: "should die" which is here interpretively rendered to mean he "should be executed," in agreement with the following Rabbinic ruling concerning this false prophet: m. Sanh. XI:5 (and b. Sanh. 89a): "'A false prophet,' he who prophesies what he has not heard, or what was not told to him, is executed by man." See also above Chap. 17, n. 8, and Gen. Chap. 44, n. 6. Similarly, Tg. Neof. and Tg. Ps.-Jon., the latter even adds "by decapitation," as well as the Syr., the Sam. Tg. (J) and the Vg. (*interficietur*).

Notes, Chapter 19

[1]See Gen. Chap. 31, n. 3.

[2]Lit. "found."

[3]Lit. "his heart is waxing hot."

[4]See n. 7 below.

[5]Lit. "spoke."

[6]See Gen. Chap. 18, n. 8.

[7]The Hebrew *dāmîm* "bloodguilt" is here expanded by the Targum who defines it as "the guilt of a judgment for murder," the very same phrase employed in vs. 6 above for the Hebrew *mišpaṭ māwet* and in Deut 22:26 for the Hebrew *ḥēṭ' māwet.* In both of the latter two cases, it is used by analogy from Deut. 21:22, where it is the exact literal equivalent for the Hebrew *ḥēṭ' mišpaṭ māwet,* and by further extension to the present verse and in 22:8 below for Hebrew *dāmîm* in an interpretive sense. The Tg. Ps.-Jon. translates similarly, while Tg. Neof. is even more explicit—"the guilt of shedding innocent blood."

[8]Lit. "the."

[9]See Exod. Chap. 23, n. 3.

is a false witness, he testified falsely against his fellowman; 19. you should do to him, as he schemed to do to his fellowman, and so remove *the evildoer*[10] from your midst. 20. The rest will hear and be afraid, and will not continue to commit such an evil act again in your midst. 21. Do not have compassion, a life for life, an eye for eye, a tooth for tooth, a hand for hand, a foot for foot.

CHAPTER 20

1. When you go out to wage war against your enemy, and you will see *horses*[1] and *chariots,*[1] a host greater than you; do not be afraid of them, for the Lord your God, who brought you out of the land of Egypt, *His Memra will be your support.*[2] 2. Then as you draw near to *engage in*[a] battle, the priest should approach and speak with the people. 3. Now he should say to them, 'Hear, O Israel! This day you are drawing near to engage your enemies in battle, let not your heart panic, do not be afraid, do not be frightened, nor be discouraged because of them. 4. For the Lord your *God*[b] will be in the lead before you, to fight the battle for you with your enemies, in order to save you.' 5. Then the officers should speak *with*[c] the people, saying, 'Who is the man that has built a new house but has not as yet dedicated it? Let him go back home, *lest he be killed*[3] in battle and another man dedicate it. 6. Who is the man who has planted a vineyard and has not as yet begun to make general use of it? Let him go back home, *lest he be killed*[3] in battle and another man begin to make general use of it. 7. Who is the man who has betrothed a woman but has not as yet married her? Let him go back home, *lest he be killed*[3] in battle and another man marry her.' 8. Thereupon the officers should continue to speak with the people saying, 'Who is the man that is afraid or fainthearted? Let him go home, lest he cause his brothers to become fainthearted like himself.' 9. When the officers have finished speaking with the people, they should appoint army commanders *to lead*[4] the people. 10. When you approach a city *to attack it,*[d] you should offer it *terms of*[5] peace. 11. Now if it responds peacefully to you and opens up <its gates> to you, all the people found in it should serve you as forced labor. 12. But if it does not communicate peacefully with you, instead engaging you in battle, then you should lay seige to it. 13. Now the Lord your God will deliver it into your control, and you should put everyone of its males to the sword. 14. Only the women, and young children, as well as the livestock and everything in the city you may plunder all as booty, and you may consume the booty of your enemy, which the Lord your God gives you. 15. So you shall deal with all the cities that are at a distance from you, and are not part of the cities

Apparatus, Chapter 20

[a] i omits; the Hebrew does not have it.
[b] So also Y, K, M, b, and c, whereas Sperber's main text inserts "His Memra" at this point.
[c] G has: "before."
[d] So also c and s, whereas Sperber's main text has: "to wage war against it."
[e] So also S, V, and c, whereas Sperber's main text has: "to wage war against it."

belonging to these nations. 16. However, in the cities of these nations that the Lord your God is giving you as an inheritance, let not a soul remain alive. 17. Instead, utterly put an end to them—the Hittites and the Amorites, the Canaanites and the Perizzites, the Hivites and the Jebusites, as the Lord your God commanded you. 18. Lest they teach you to imitate all their abominable acts that they practice before their *idols,*[6] and you will sin *before*[7] the Lord your God. 19. When you lay siege to a city for a long time in order *to attack it*[e] and (to) conquer it, do not destroy its tree<s> by wielding the ax over it, because you may eat from it, so do not cut it down; *since trees of the field are not like humans,*[8] to be included by you in a siege. 20. Except for a tree which you know is not a *food tree,*[9] you may destroy; it you may cut down; and you should construct siege-works against the city that is waging war on you, until you have conquered it.

CHAPTER 21

1. If a corpse is found strewn in the field within the land that the Lord your God is giving you to possess, and it is not known who killed him, 2. your elders and your judges should go out and measure {the distance} from the corpse to the surrounding cities. 3. Now the elders of that city, the one which is nearest to the corpse, should take a heifer of the herd which has never been worked, which has never pulled in a yoke. 4. Then the

Notes, Chapter 19 (Cont.)

[10]See above Chap. 13, n. 7.

Notes, Chapter 20

[1]See Gen. Chap. 21, n. 7.
[2]See Gen. Chap. 26, n. 2.
[3]The Hebrew has: "lest he die," which is here interpretively rendered to mean "killed." See Gen. Chap. 26, n. 6. Tg. Ps.-Jon. and the Syr. translate similarly here, as does the Sam. Tg. (J).
[4]Lit. "at the head of."
[5]An insertion implied in the Hebrew.
[6]See Introduction VII A.3.
[7]See Gen. Chap. 4, n. 1.
[8]The Hebrew constitutes a rhetorical question which the Targum transforms into the corresponding negative statement. So also the Syr., Tgs. Ps.-Jon., and Neof., as well as the Vg.; whereas the LXX keeps the rhetorical tone of the Hebrew.
[9]Lit. "a tree for food."

elders of that city should bring the heifer down to the *untilled*[1] valley, that *will not be*[a2] plowed or sown, and there in the valley, they should strike down the heifer mortally. 5. Thereupon the priests, the descendants of *Levi,*[b] should approach, for the Lord your God has chosen them to serve Him and to pronounce a blessing in the name of the Lord; and every dispute and every case of a *leprosy plague*[3] is subject to their *ruling.*[4] 6. Now all the elders of that city which is nearest to the corpse, should wash their hands over the heifer that was mortally struck down in the valley. 7. Then they should declare, saying, 'Our hands did not shed his blood, nor did our eyes see it <done>' 8. *The priests should* <then> *respond;*[5] 'O Lord, forgive your people Israel whom You have redeemed, and let not the *guilt for*[c6] the blood of the innocent be placed upon your people Israel, and they will be forgiven for the blood <shed>' 9. Now you should remove from your midst *those who shed*[d6] the blood of the innocent, for you will be doing what is proper *before*[7] the Lord. 10. When you go out to *wage*[8] war against your enemies, and the Lord your God will deliver them in your hand, and you will take some of them captives, 11. and you will see among the captives a beautiful looking woman, and you will desire her and will take her for a wife, 12. you should bring her into your house, and she should shave her head *and let her nails grow* <*wild*>.[9] 13. Then she should remove her captivity garment from herself and stay in your house, where she should mourn her father and her mother for a month's time; thereafter you may go to her and be her husband and she shall be your wife. 14. Thereafter, if you no longer desire her, you must release her to her own rights but you may in no way sell her for money; you may not use her as merchandise, since you have afflicted her. 15. If a man has two wives, one beloved, the

Apparatus, Chapter 21

[a] l has the perfect: "has not been," whereas i has the participle: "is not."

[b] b and g have: "the Levites."

[c] d_2 has: "shedding of."

[d] G has: "the guilt of."

Notes, Chapter 21

[1]The Hebrew has: *'ēṯān* which the Targum, as well as Tgs. Neof. and Ps.-Jon., and the Syr. all render by the identical Aramaic term *byyr* "untilled," "waste" (only the Sam. Tg. differs by using *'myq*—"deep"). The LXX and Vg. contain translations which show an understanding of the word as it exists in Num. 24:21 where it is in synonymous parallelism to Hebrew *séla'* "rock," consequently the LXX has *τραχεῖαν*—"rocky," and the Vg. *asperam atque saxosam*—"rough and rocky." This is also the understanding of this word in Rabbinic literature: m. Sot. IX:5 (also b. Sot. 45b) and Sifre *Šôpṭîm* CCVII, p. 242—"*'ēṯān* is to be understood in its literal sense of 'hard', even if it not be stony." S.R. Driver (*Deuteronomy: ICC.* Edinburgh, 1929, p. 242), however points out that the real meaning of the word is "ever-flowing, perennial" from the Arabic *watana*—"to be constant" especially of water. Thus *náḥal 'êtān* in the present verse would mean a "torrent-valley," a stream (= *náḥal,* rather than a "ravine") in which water flowed continuously. This is precisely the meaning that Maimonides (Mishneh Torah: Laws concerning the Murderer Chap. 9:2) used in translating this phrase—"a stream that flows intensely." Cf. also Ps. 74:15 where *'êtān* occurs with the term for "streams."

[2]The text of Vat. 448 is here a literal translation of the Hebrew, rendering both verbs—"plow" and "sow" in the imperfect, so also Tg. Ps.-Jon., whereas the Syr., the Sam. Tg., and to some extent Tg. Neof. have the perfect form of these verbs, as does the Vg. and one Onq. ms. (for which cf. Apparatus, note *a*). The LXX has the perfect for the first verb and the participle for the second, and one Onq. ms. has the participle for both verbs (see Apparatus, note *a*). The Mishnah (m. Sot. IX:5) has: "the site may never be sown or tilled" which is clear in the imperfect, however, the Talmud thereafter (b. Sot. 46b) records the following dispute on the matter: "The site may never be sown or tilled. Our Rabbis taught 'which is neither plowed or sown'

other hated, and the beloved one and the hated one bore him sons, but the firstborn is the son of the hated one—16. Now the day he wills his possessions to his sons, he is not permitted to grant firstborn status to the son of the beloved one, in preference to the son of the hated one, the actual firstborn. 17. Instead he must *set aside*[10] the firstborn son of the hated one and assign to him two *portions*[11] of all that he has, for he is the beginning of his strength, the birthright is duly his. 18. If a man has a defiant and rebellious son

Notes, Chapter 21 (Cont.)

(Deut. 21:4)—this refers to the past; such is the statement of R. Josiah. R. Jonathan says: It refers to the future. Raba said: Nobody disputes as to the future since it is written: 'it shall not be sown,' where they differ is to the past, R. Josiah argues: Is it written, '*And it* shall not be tilled'? ('which will not be tilled' is written. [addition according to the Bach]). And R. Jonathan argues: Is it written, 'Which *has not been* tilled'? (therefore it must refer to the future). And (how does) R. Josiah (meet R. Jonathan's argument)? The relative pronoun *which* (Hebrew *'ăšer*) must be understood of the past (since it would not be used if a command were implied, in which case the verse would have stated 'it shall not be tilled'). And R. Jonathan? *Which* is employed in an inclusive sense."

[3]See above Chap. 17, n. 6.

[4]Lit. "word."

[5]An insertion, also present in Tgs. Neof. and Ps.-Jon. and in Sifre (*ibid.*, CCX, p. 244): "The priests say: Forgive your people Israel," as well as in m. Sot. IX:5.

[6]An insertion to resolve the figurative Hebrew. As pointed out in the Apparatus (note *c*) a variant has "shedding of" which serves the same purpose though not as patently as does "guilt for." Tg. Ps.-Jon. has "guilt for," whereas Tg. Neof. has both—"the guilt for the shedding of." The same situation holds true in the following verse.

[7]The Targum here employs the particle *qdm* to avoid the anthropomorphism of the Hebrew.

[8]See Num. Chap. 10, n. 1.

[9]The Hebrew has: "and do her nails." This interpretive translation of the Targum is in agreement with Rabbi Aqiba, whose dispute with Rabbi Eliezer in the matter is detailed in Sifre (*Kî Tēṣē'* CCXII, p. 245) and b. Yeb. 48a: "Our Rabbis taught: 'And she should shave her head and do her nails' (Deut. 21:12). R. Eliezer said: She shall cut them (the nails). Rabbi Aqiba said: She shall grow them. R. Eliezer said: An act was mentioned in respect of the head, and an act was mentioned in respect of the nails; as the former signifies removal, so the latter also signifies removal. R. Aqiba said: An act was mentioned in respect of the head, and an act was mentioned in respect of the nails; as disfigurement is the purpose of the former, so is disfigurement the purpose of the latter. The following, however, supports the view of R. Eliezer—'And Mephibosheth, the son of Saul, came down to meet the king, and he had neither dressed his feet nor had he done his beard' (2 Sam. 19:25); by 'doing' *removal* was meant."

[10]The Hebrew has: "acknowledge," which the LXX (ἐπιγνώσεται), the Sam. Tg. (*ykr*), and Tg. Neof. m_1 (*yštmwd'*) render literally, while the Vg. (*agnoscet primogenitum*—"acknowledge his primogeniture") and Tg. Ps.-Jon. ("acknowledge to all that he is the firstborn") go a step further, the latter being identical to the opening statement mentioned in Sifre (*ibid.* CCXVII, p. 250). The Syr. omits translating the word, while Tg. Neof. has "bring close" (*qrb*) and Tg. Neof. m_2 has "give preference to (*qdm*)." The use of *prš* by the Targum in translating Hebrew *ykyr* to mean "set aside" may be his way of succinctly reflecting the Rabbinic interpretation mentioned in Sifre (and also contained in a variety of other Rabbinic sources) as follows: "he should acknowledge him before others, teaching that a man is believed to declare: 'This is my firstborn son.'" By "setting him aside" he accomplishes this commandment, whereas the use of the literal *yštmwd'* (as in Tg. Neof. m_1) would imply that only he acknowledges him. That is precisely the reason for Tg. Ps.-Jon. to have inserted—"to all" in his translation of this word. Cf. also the following: b.Qidd. 74a and 78b; b. B. Bat. 127b; b. Yeb. 47a; Bereshit Rabbati XXXV:23, p. 158, and Aggadath Bereshit XLIX:3, p. 98.

[11]The Hebrew *pî* is here rendered by its secondary derivative meaning "portions," the Targum using the term *ḥlq* in the plural as in the following Midrashic interpretation of this passage—Tanḥ(A) *Wayěḥî* IX "The additional amount of the 'birthright' is in the form of two portions (*ḥlqym*), as it says: 'to allot to him a double portion' (Deut. 21:17)."

who does not *obey the command of*[12] his father *or the command of*[12] his mother, even though they teach him, he does not listen to them, 19. his father and his mother shall take hold of him and bring him out before the elders of his city, and to the entrance of *the courthouse of*[13] his district. 20. Then they should say to the elders of his city, 'This son of ours is defiant and rebellious, he does not *obey our command;*[12] he is a glutton *with meat*[14] and a drunkard *with wine.*'[14] 21. Thereupon all the men of his city should stone him to death, that you may remove *the evildoer*[15] from your midst, and all of Israel will hear and be afraid. 22. If a man, *who is condemned to die,*[16] is put to death, and you impale him on a stake, 23. you must not leave his corpse on the stake overnight, but you must surely bury him that very day, *because he was impaled for having sinned before the Lord;*[17] and you must not defile the land that the Lord your God is giving you <as> an inherited possession.

CHAPTER 22

1. If you see your fellowman's ox or his sheep going astray, do not ignore them; be sure to return them to your fellowman. 2. If your fellowman *does not live*[1] near you or you do not know him, you should bring it into your house, where it should remain with you until your fellowman claims it, and you should give it back to him. 3. Now you should do likewise with his donkey, and you should do likewise with his garment, and do likewise with all the lost articles belonging to your fellowman that he may have lost and you find them; you are not permitted to conceal it. 4. If you see your fellowman's donkey or his ox fallen on the road, do not ignore them, but be sure to help raise it up. 5. A woman should not wear a man's *armament*[2] nor should a man put on a woman's *ornaments;*[2] for whoever does these things *is abhorrent before*[3] the Lord your God. 6. If

Apparatus, Chapter 22

[a] b and g have: "the guilt of a judgment for murder." See above Chap. 19, n. 7.

Notes, Chapter 21 (Cont.)

[12]See Gen. Chap. 3, n. 9.

[13]The Targum here associates Hebrew *šá'ar* ("gate") with the Beth Din (court), an association commonly made in Rabbinic literature, as can be seen from the following discussion in the Talmud (b. Ket. 45b): "... from what our Rabbis have taught: (By the expression) 'your gates' (Deut. 17:5) was meant the gate (of the city) wherein the man has worshiped. You say the gate (of the city) wherein the man has worshiped, might it not mean the gate where he is tried (as the judges' seat was at the city gate (for which cf. Ruth 4:1ff.)..." With regard to Deut. 17:5, the Talmud (*ibid.*) had earlier stated "A man who worships idols is to be stoned at the gate of the city where he worshiped, and in a city, the majority of whose inhabitants are idolaters, he is stoned at the entrance of the court." Cf. also t. Sanh. X:10, and Sifre *Šôptîm* CXLVIII, p. 202, and CXLIX, p. 204 for similar "gate" - "court" associations. Tgs. Neof. and Ps.-Jon. render identically to Tg. Onq. here.

you chance upon a bird's nest along the road, in any tree or on the ground, fledglings or eggs, and the mother is sitting on the fledglings or on the eggs, do not take the mother together with the young. 7. Be sure to <first> send away the mother and <then> take the young for yourself, so that you fare well and have a long life. 8. When you build a new house, you should make a parapet for your roof, so that you do not bring *the guilt of murder*[a4] on your house caused by the fall of anyone who fell from it. 9. Do not plant a mixture of seeds in your vineyard, lest the *fruit of*[5] the seed that you planted and the

Notes, Chapter 21 (Cont.)

[14]These insertions, applying gluttony to meat and drunkenness to wine, are specifically spelled out in the following Mishna (m. Sanh. VIII:2, cf. also b. Sanh. 70a and 71a): "If he ate any food but meat *or* drank any drink but wine, he does not become a 'defiant and rebellious son' thereby, unless he eats meat *and* drinks wine, for it is written '(this our son is defiant and rebellious, he will not obey our voice), he is a glutton (*zôlēl*) *and* a drunkard (*wĕsōḇē'*) [Deut. 21:20]. And though there is no absolute proof, there is a suggestion for it, as it is written 'Be not among winebibbers (*bĕ-sôḇ'ē*) nor among gluttonous eaters of flesh' (Prov. 23:20)." Cf. further Sifre (*Kî Tēṣē'* CCXIX, p. 252) and Tanḥ(A) *Šĕmînî* V.

[15]See above Chap. 13, n. 7.

[16]See above Chap. 19, n. 7.

[17]The Hebrew "for he that is impaled is under the curse of God" is here paraphrased in order to avoid associating the notion of curse with God. The Targum circumvents this association by first translating generally "sinned" in place of "curse" and then associating the act of sinning with man before (*qdm*) God. Similarly, the Midrash, though here the act of cursing—blasphemy—is retained but attributed to man—Sifre (*ibid.* CCXXI, p. 254) "'for he that is impaled is under the curse of God' (Deut. 21:23), that is to say, why is this one being impaled? Because he cursed the Name, which resulted in the desecration of the Name of Heaven." The other Aramaic Versions likewise attempt to circumvent this problem by a variety of paraphrases, thus Tg. Ps.-Jon. "because it is a disgrace before God to impale someone unless his sins were the cause of it;" Tg. Neof. "because anyone who is impaled, is accursed before the Lord;" and the Syr. "for he who reviles God shall be impaled." Cf. also Num. Rab. VIII:4 and y. Qidd. IV:1, p. 65c, where the sin of the impaled one in this verse is described as "desecration of the Name of God," and y. Naz. VII:1, p. 55d where the sin is "blasphemy."

Notes, Chapter 22

[1]Lit. "is not."

[2]The Hebrew has: "... (man's) apparel ... (woman's) clothing ..." This interpretive rendering in the Targum, according to which Hebrew *kly* refers to "armament," and *śimlat* to "ornaments," precisely reflects the opinion of Rabbi Eliezer b. Jacob cited in Sifre (*Kî Tēṣē'* CCXXVI, p. 258) and the following Talmud (b. Naz. 59a): "Rabbi Eliezer b. Jacob says: How do we know that a woman should not go to war bearing arms? Scripture says: 'A woman should not wear that which pertains to a man' (Deut. 22:5). (The words) 'neither should a man put on a woman's garment' (*ibid.*) signify that a man is not to use cosmetics as women do."

[3]The Hebrew "is an abhorrence of" is here paraphrased in order to avoid the direct association of the notion of abhorrence with God in a genitive phrase. Instead the noun abhorrence is converted into the corresponding adjective and *qdm* is inserted before God's name.

[4]See above Chap. 19, n. 7.

[5]The Hebrew, *hamĕlē'āh* ("the full produce"), according to the syntax could conceivably be taken as the direct object of the preceding verb *tiqdaš* (active in form, but passive in sense), the following clause "the seed which you have sown" would, as S.R. Driver (*Deuteronomy: ICC, op. cit.*, p. 252f) correctly points out, "define more distinctly what is intended by *hamĕlē'āh.*" The Targum, however, combines *hamĕlē'āh* with the immediately following *hazzéra'* into a genitive phrase, translating the former by *dim'at* "fruit of" and the latter literally "the seed," the entire phrase being governed by the verb *tiqdaš* here rendered into a passive. This interpretive approach of the Targum was no doubt precipitated by the grammatical problem that the Hebrew could present with the two words *hamĕlē'āh* and *hazzéra'*. What is the connection between the two? In fact, according to the Talmud they cannot be one as they appear to be the antithesis of each other, as

produce of the vineyard become *defiled.*[6] 10. Do not plow with an ox and a donkey <yoked> together. 11. Do not wear *ša'atnēs*—clothes of wool and linen *joined*[7] together. 12. You should make *tassels*[8] on the four corners of *the*[9] garments with which you cover yourself. 13. If a man takes a wife and cohabits with her, and then takes on a dislike for her, 14. by claiming false charges against her and spreading a bad name about her, saying, 'I married this woman when I sexually *went up to*[b] her, I did not find <proof of> her virginity.' 15. Then the girl's father and her mother should produce the <evidence of> the girl's virginity before the elders of the city *at the entrance of the court of that district.*[10] 16. And the girl's father should say to the elders, 'I gave my daughter to this man as a wife, and he took a dislike to her, 17. and he has claimed false charges, saying: I did not find your daughter to be a virgin; but here is proof of my daughter's virginity,' and they should spread out *the cloth*[11] before the elders of the city. 18. Then the elders of that city should take the man and *flog*[12] him, 19. and they should fine him a hundred silver *selas*[13] and *pay*[14] {these} to the girl's father, since he has spread a bad name about a virgin *daughter of*[c] Israel; therefore she should *remain*[15] his wife; he is never permitted to divorce her. 20. But if this claim proves to be true, the girl was found not to have been a virgin, 21. then they should bring out the girl to the entrance of her father's house, *where*[d] the people of the city should stone her to death, since she committed a shameful act in Israel by being promiscuous <while in> her father's house, and so you will remove *the evildoer*[16] from your midst. 22. If a man is found lying with another man's wife, both of them—the man who was lying with the woman and the woman—should *be executed,*[e] and so you will remove *the evildoer*[16] from your midst. 23. If a man found a virgin girl who was betrothed to another man in the city and lay with her, 24. you should bring both of them out to the gate of that city, and they should stone them to death; the girl because she did not cry out <for help> in the city, and the man because he violated his fellowman's wife; and so you will remove *the evildoer*[16] from your midst. 25. But if the man *found the betrothed girl*[f] in the field, and the man overpowered her and lay with her; then, only the man who lay with her should *be executed,*[e] 26. but nothing should be done to the girl; the girl is not guilty *to be condemned to*[17] death, for this case is like one where a person rose up against another and killed that person; 27. for the man found her in the field, the betrothed girl cried out <for help> but there was no one who saved her. 28. If a man found a virgin girl who was not betrothed, and he seized her and lay with her, whereupon they are discovered—

Apparatus, Chapter 22 (Cont.)

[b] D and i have: "approached," as does the Hebrew.

[c] M, c, and s omit; the Hebrew does not have it.

[d] j and l add: "all," as do many Cairo Geniza Hebrew mss., as well as some Kennicott readings.

[e] D has: "die," as does the Hebrew.

[f] b has: "is found (with the betrothed girl)."

29. The man who laid with her should *pay*[14] a fine of fifty silver *selas*[13] to the father of the girl, and she shall become his wife; because he had violated her, he is never permitted to divorce her.

Notes, Chapter 22 (Cont.)

seen from the following discussion in b. Ḥul. 116a and b. Pes. 25a (the latter of which is hereby cited, the former differing only in minor details). "Raba said: There are two texts, it is written 'the fullness' (*hamĕlē'āh*) and 'the seed' is written. How is this (to be reconciled)?" The question here being that "the fullness" implies the additional growth only, while "the seed" implies the original stock. By combining the two into a genitive construction, the Targum thus resolved these questions. Tg. Ps.-Jon. parallels Onq. here, while Tg. Neof. renders the Hebrew literally, yet by a genitive construction.

[6]The Hebrew has: *tiqdaš*, lit. "forfeit to the sanctuary," which the Targum renders interpretively "defiled." Rashi, who translates this word as the Targum does, attempts to reconcile the two terms by explaining *tiqdaš* to be understood as meaning "unfit for use" as Hebrew *qdš* can apply to anything for which man has repugnance *to come into contact with,* be it on account of its sublimity, as for instance, sacred matter, or be it on account of some bad quality, as for instance, something that is forbidden; in both instances the term *qdš* is appropriate, as *in the latter sense,* e.g., (Isa. 65:5) "Come not near to me for I make you *qdwš*.'" The Tg. Ps.-Jon. renders *tqdš* "(lest the fruit of the seed) will have to be burned" which is in direct agreement with the Rabbinic interpretation of this word in the Talmud (b. Qidd. 56b and b. Ḥul. 115a) "'*pen tiqdaš'* -*pen tiqdaš 'ēš*—lest it be burned in fire' (in b. Qidd. it is attributed to the Tanna Hezekiah)." Tg. Neof. translates *tiqdaš* as "destroy" (< *'bd*).

[7]The insertion of this term in the Targum reflects the halakhic point of view that the prohibition of wearing *ša'atnēz* involves a garment in which the wool and linen had to be intertwined in some way, as can be seen from the following Rabbinic texts:

1. *b. Yeb. 5b* "Scripture should have stated: 'You shall not wear a mingled stuff (*ša'atnēz*), wool and linen' (Deut. 22:11) what need was there to add 'together'? . . . for the deduction that two stitches (combining a material made of wool with one made of linen) form a combination, and that one stitch does not! If so, the All Merciful should have written: 'You shall not wear wool and linen together'; what need was there for inserting 'mingled stuff'? . . . for the deduction that 'mingled stuff' is not forbidden unless it was hackled, spun, and twisted." Cf. further Sifre (*ibid.* CCXXXII, p. 265; Sifra *Qĕdôšîm* II:4, p. 89; and PRE XXI.) Tgs. Neof. and Ps.-Jon. add "mixed" (*'rb*).

[8]See Num. Chap. 15, n. 12.

[9]Lit. "your."

[10]See above Chap. 21, n. 13.

[11]The Hebrew has: "garment" which is here rendered by the Aramaic *šwšyp'*—"cloth" in place of the literal *ksw* as in Deut. 10:18, to emphasize R. Eliezer b. Jacob's opinion as expressed in the Talmud (as well as in Sifre [*ibid.* CCXXXVII, p. 269f.])—b. Ket. 46a: ". . . as it was taught: 'and they shall spread the garment' (Deut. 22:17) teaches that the witnesses of the one party and those of the other party come, *and the matter is made clear as a new garment.* R. Eliezer b. Jacob said: The words are to be taken in their literal sense: (they must produce) the actual garment." Tg. Ps.-Jon. here parallels Onq., whereas Tg. Neof., the Syr., the Sam. Tg., and the Vg. have: "beat."

[12]The Hebrew has: "punish" (*yisrû*), which the Targum here interpretively renders "flog" directly reflecting Rabbinic opinion expressed in Sifre (*ibid.* CCXXXVIII, p. 270): 'and they should punish him' (Deut. 22:18)—with stripes;" cf. also b. Ket. 46a; b. Sanh. 71b; y. Ter. VII:1, p. 44c; y. Ket. III:1, p. 27b.

[13]See Gen. Chap. 20, n. 11.

[14]Lit. "give."

[15]Lit. "be."

[16]See above Chap. 13, n. 7.

[17]An insertion by analogy from Deut. 21:22, where the full phrase *ḥēt' mišpaṭ mówet* occurs, whereas here the middle element is missing in the Hebrew but supplied in the Targum. See further above Chap. 19, n. 7.

CHAPTER 23

1. A man should not marry his father's wife and so not reveal his father's *shame.*[1] 2. No one whose testicles have been crushed or whose testicles have been *severed*[a] is *considered purified for admission*[2] into the congregation of the Lord. 3. Neither is a bastard *considered purified for admission*[2] into the congregation of the Lord, even in the tenth generation will he not be *considered purified* for *admission*[2] into the congregation of the Lord. 4. The Ammonites and the Moabites are not *considered purified for admission*[2] into the congregation of the Lord, 5. because they did not come to meet you with bread and water on the road after you departed from Egypt, but rather hired Balaam, son of Beor, from Aram *on the Euphrates,*[3] to curse you. 6. But the Lord did not want to *listen to*[4] Balaam; instead the Lord your God turned the curses into blessings for you, because the Lord your God loves you. 7. Do not advocate their welfare or their prosperity as long as you live. 8. Do not abhor an Edomite for he is your kinsman; do not abhor an Egyptian for you were an alien in his land. 9. Children born to them in the third generation will be *considered purified,*[2] for them to enter the congregation of the Lord. 10. When you go out as a troop against your enemies, guard yourself against anything improper. 11. If anyone among you has been rendered unclean because of a nocturnal emission, he should go outside the confines of the camp and may not re-enter the camp. 12. Then *toward*[b] evening he should bathe in water, and at sunset may re-enter the confines of the camp. 13. Moreover, you should have a *designated place*[5] for you outside the camp, *where you go*[6] <to relieve yourself>. 14. *With*[c] your equipment you should have a spike; then after *you have relieved yourself,*[7] you should turn back and cover up your excrement. 15. For the Lord your God, His *Shekhinah*[8] moves about in your camp, to help you, and to deliver your enemies *before you;*[d] therefore your camp should be sacred so that *He will not notice among you anything offensive*[e] and *the Memra*[9] turn away from *favoring*[10] you. 16. You should not deliver the slave *of the heathens*[11] to *the hand of*[f] his master, who has come to seek refuge by

Apparatus, Chapter 23

[a] I adds: "and one whose load was severed;" while n adds: "and one <whose testicles> were severed and torn loose," as in Lev. 22:24.
[b] D has: "at the time of."
[c] I has: "in addition to."
[d] D has: "in your hand."
[e] D, G, and v have: "nothing offensive will be noticed among you."
[f] k and I omit; the Hebrew does not have it.
[g] D omits, as does c; the Hebrew does not have it.
[h] I has: "be."

you from *before*[g] his master. 17. He should *live*[h] with you, among you, in any place he so chooses within your *cities,*[12] wherever he pleases; do not mistreat him. 18. *An Israelite woman may not marry a male slave, and an Israelite male may not marry a female*

Notes, Chapter 23

[1]Lit. "skirt," euphemistically used as in Ezek. 16:8 and Ruth 3:9.

[2]The Hebrew has: "permitted to come." This interpretive rendering of the Targum which introduces the notion of purity into the situation, reflects the following Mishnah, where this phrasing is similarly used with regards to permitting bastards to marry, m. Qidd. III:13 "R. Tarfon said: *Mamzerim* ('bastards') can be purified. How? If a Mamzer marries a bondwoman ..." Likewise b. Qidd. 71a "R. Joshua B. Levi said: Money purifies *Mamzerim,*" meaning because of their wealth they intermarry with Israel. Thus the "considered purified" applies to the idea of marriage here, and, although the above-cited text deals with "bastards" here mentioned in vs. 3, the translation was applied to vss. 2 and 4 as well. Tg. Ps.-Jon. is even more explicit in rendering "considered purified to marry a woman." Cf. also b. Qidd. 69a "*Mamzerim* could become purified."

[3]See Gen. Chap. 24, n. 3.

[4]See Gen. Chap. 16, n. 1.

[5]The Hebrew *yād* is here rendered interpretively—"a designated place" a translation paralleled in Tgs. Ps.-Jon. and Neof. and virtually in the Syr., the Sam. Tg., the Vg., and the LXX, all of whom have simply "place." This translation is reflected in Sifre (*Kî Tēṣē'* CCLVII, p. 281): "'Furthermore there should be for you a *yād* outside the camp' (Deut. 23:13). *Yād* means nothing else but place, as it says (1 Sam. 15:12) 'there he set up a place for him,' and (Num. 2:17) 'each at his place, by their standards.'"

[6]Lit. "and there you should go outside."

[7]Lit. "you have squatted outside."

[8]See Introduction VII D. 3.

[9]See Introduction VII D. 1.

[10]The Hebrew has: "and turn away from you." The Targum here injects the Memra, which will be involved in "turning away" (for which see Gen. Chap. 3, n. 4), and then adds: "from favoring." A similar situation, but in reverse, exists in Lev. 26:9 where the Hebrew has: "and I will turn towards you" which the Targum there renders "and I will turn with My Memra to favor you;" see there n. 6.

[11]The Hebrew has simply: "slave" which the Targum renders interpretively to refer to a slave of the heathens. The question now arises as to whether this is a Hebrew slave sold to the heathens, or a genuine heathen slave. Most commentaries (Adler, *Netina La-Ger, op. cit.,* on this verse; Schefftel, *Bi'ure Onqelos, op. cit.,* p. 256; Berkowitz, *Liwyat Ḥên* in *Avne Ẕiyon.* Wilna, 1877, p. 58) as well as Rashi's second explanation where he cites b. Git. 45a, take it to mean a heathen slave belonging to a heathen who fled from abroad to the land of Israel. P. Churgin ("The Halakha in Targum Onqelos" [in Hebrew], *Talpiyot* 2 [1945-46]: p. 429), however, favors the likelihood that it is an Israelite slave who was sold to a heathen. This opinion is shared by Berkowitz (*Simlat Ger* in *Leḥem WeSimla.* Wilna, 1850-55, p. 36) who reasons that had it meant a genuine heathen slave it would have said *bar 'ammemîn,* the presence of *bar* being critical here as it appears in Exod. 21:2 where an Israelite slave is specifically designated as *bar yisrā'ēl.* The Sifre (*ibid.* CCLIX, p. 282) contains both possibilities:

1. "'You should not deliver a slave to his master' (Deut. 23:16) from here it is said that one who sells his slave to heathens or abroad, he goes out free." This would imply that the slave is Hebrew.

2. Another explanation: 'You should not deliver a slave to his master,' the verse speaks about a heathen who was saved from idolatry."

Tg. Ps.-Jon., however, clearly identifies the slave as a heathen—"... an uncircumcised slave into the hands of idolators."

[12]See Gen. Chap. 22, n. 13.

slave.[13] 19. You may not bring the fee of a prostitute or the *exchange*[14] for a dog into the *Temple*[i] of the Lord your God <in fulfillment> of any vow; for both of them are indeed *abhorrent before*[j] the Lord your God. 20. Do not charge *interest*[15] from your fellowman, be it *interest*[15] in money, *interest*[15] in *produce,*[16] *interest*[15] in anything whatsoever that *is*[k] deducted as *interest.*[15] 21. You may charge *interest*[15] to foreigners, but you may not charge *interest*[15] to your kinsman, so that the Lord your God may bless you in all your undertakings, in the land which you are about to enter and take possession of it. 22. When you make a vow before the Lord *your God,*[l] do not delay in fulfilling it, for the Lord your God will surely demand it from you, and you will have incurred guilt. 23. But if you refrain from making vows you will incur no guilt. 24. You should fulfill what has crossed your lips, and do what you have vowed to do *before*[17] the Lord your God, having made the promise with your own mouth. 25. *If you become a hired laborer*[18] in your fellowman's vineyard, you may eat grapes to your personal satisfaction, but do not put <any> into your vessel. 26. *If you become a hired laborer*[18] in your fellowman's standing grain <field> you may pluck kernels with your hand, but do not put a sickle to your fellowman's standing grain.

Apparatus, Chapter 23 (Cont.)

[i] D has: "house," as does the Hebrew.
[j] D has: "an abhorrence of," as does the Hebrew.
[k] C and M have: "could be."
[l] I omits.

Notes, Chapter 23 (Cont.)

[13]The Hebrew has: "No Israelite woman should be a cult prostitute, nor should any Israelite man be a cult prostitute." The Targum here departs radically from the Hebrew text by translating it to apply to the ban on marriage between Israelites and slaves in both male and female combination. Rashi citing the Targum here, attempts to harmonize the latter's translation with the Hebrew text by reasoning that when the Targum translates the first half of this verse—"a woman of the daughters of Israel shall not become the wife of a slave"; such a woman may also be termed a ***qĕdēšāh*** (Hebrew word for "prostitute" here) because she too becomes a prostitute to illicit intercourse, since no marriage ceremony with her is valid for him.... Likewise the second half of this verse, which the Targum renders "no Israelite son should marry a bondwoman" is an adequate translation, since he, too, becomes a *qādēš*, "one devoted to illicit intercourse "through her, since every intercourse with her is illicit; so no marriage ceremony with her can be valid for him. Churgin (*Talpiyot* 2 *op. cit.*, p. 430) theorizes that the Targum's wide digression here was intentionally aimed at the intermarriage between the Hasmoneans and the Herodians, the latter of which were regarded as descendants of Idumaean slaves. Z. Markon (*Mi-Sifrotenu Ha-Atiqa.* Wilna, 1910, p. 15) is convinced that the digression is related to the preceding verse which deals with a heathen slave (see n. 10 above), concerning whom it is said "He should live with you in any place he may choose among the settlements in your midst." The next verse then points out that although he may live with you anywhere he so chooses, but marriage is out. Maimonides (*'Isûrê Bî'āh* II:13) points to the Onqelos rendering of this verse. Cf. Berliner, *Targum Onkelos: Einleitung..., op. cit.*, p. 242, who correctly points to b. Qidd. 75b "the child resulting from a sexual act between a slave and an Israelite woman is a Mamzer" as paralleling the Targum here.

[14]The Hebrew has: *mĕḥîr* ("price") which the Targum rendered by the interpretive translation "exchange," one that is reflected in the Talmud (b. Tem. 30a): "Our Rabbis have taught: 'A *mĕḥîr* of a dog' (Deut. 23:19), this refers to that taken in exchange for the dog." Likewise Sifre (*ibid.* CCLXI, p. 283) "A *mĕḥîr* of a dog" (Deut. 23:19). What is considered 'a *mĕḥîr* of a dog'? If one says to his fellowman: Take this lamb in exchange for this dog." The Pal. Tgs. including the Frg. Tg. (V), Neof. and Ps.-Jon. all have *pîrûg* which Jastrow (*op. cit.*, p. 1170) renders "exchange," "price."

[15]The Hebrew has the word *nĕšeḵ* as the noun and *taššîḵ* its corresponding verbal form throughout this passage, which the Targum renders by the term *ribbîṯ* and its corresponding verbal form < *rby.* Both forms

CHAPTER 24

1. If a man marries a woman and has sexual relations with her, but she fails to please him because he finds something offensive about her; he may write her *a bill of dismissal,*[1] hand it to her, and send her away from his house. 2. Then after she leaves his house she marries another man. 3. If the latter husband rejects her and writes her *a bill of dismissal,*[1] hands it to her, and sends her away from his house; or if the latter husband

Notes, Chapter 23 (Cont.)

mean "interest," however the Rabbis set forth a clear distinction between ***néšek̠*** and *ribbît/tarbit/marbit* (for which cf. m. B. Meṣ. V:1, also b. B.Meṣ. 60b) with the former, from the root ***nšk*** "to bite," denoting usury, something "bitten out" from the debtor, something received for nothing given; whereas the latter from the root *rby*—"to increase" denotes just that—"increase," "profits." Both terms occur in Lev. 25:36, 37, whereas here only ***nšk*** occurs and is rendered by *rby* in an interpretive sense throughout. In Lev. 25:36, 37, the Targum renders Hebrew *tarbît* and *marbît* by *ribbitā',* and Hebrew *néšek̠* by *ḥibbûlyā',* in order to avoid duplication of the root *rby.*

[16]See Gen. Chap. 41, n. 14.

[17]See Gen. Chap. 4, n. 1.

[18]The Hebrew has: "when you come" which could mean anyone, and not just a hired laborer as the Targum translates it. This subject was the center of a dispute in the Talmud (b. B. Meṣ. 92a) where one Issi b. Judah interpreted "When you come into your fellowman's vineyard" (Deut. 23:25) as referring "to the coming of any man" (not only a hired laborer). "Whereupon Rab commented: Issi makes life impossible for anyone" (social life is impossible if any person may enter and eat of one's crop). Now the first Tanna of the preceding Mishnah agrees with Rab (and that appears to be the consensus throughout those sections where these two verses are discerned (cf. *ibid.,* p. 87b, 88b, 89a, 91b), and says only a hired laborer may eat, etc. This opinion is also expressed in Sifre (*ibid.* CCLXVI, p. 286) "'When you come into your fellowman's vineyard' (Deut. 23:25). I would say always, therefore it says, 'but do not put any into your vessel' (*ibid.*), (only) at the time when you put (some) into the owner's vessel."

"'When you come into your fellowman's standing corn <field> ' (Deut. 23:26). I would say always, therefore it says 'but do not put a sickle' (*ibid.*), (only) at the time when you put a sickle to the standing corn of the owner."

The Targum then follows the Rabbinic tradition of Rab set forth in the above-cited Talmud (b. B. Meṣ.) and the Sifre passage, according to which these two verses speak only of a hired laborer and not just any man. Even more explicit on this point is the Jerusalem Talmud, of which the following have been selected for citation:

y. Ma'aś. II:6, p. 50a "It is written: 'When you come into the standing corn <field> of your fellowman' (Deut. 23:26), I would think the verse is speaking of any type of person, therefore it says: 'but do not put the sickle to the standing corn of your fellowman' (*ibid.*)—only the one who has permission to put the sickle (to the standing corn) and who is this, the hired worker."

Ibid.:7 "It is written: 'When you come into the vineyard of your fellowman' (Deut. 23:25), I would think the verse is speaking of any type of person, therefore it says: 'but do not put <any> into your vessel' (*ibid.*) but you may put (some) into the vessel of your fellowman, and who is this, the hired laborer."

Notes, Chapter 24

[1]The Hebrew *sép̄er kĕrîtût*—lit. "a document of separation," is here rendered by one of three technical phrases employed in Rabbinic literature—*get pittûrîn*—"a bill of dismissal," the other two, *sēp̄er tērûkîn*—"a writ of divorce," and *'iggéret šĕb̠ûqîn*—"a letter of release," are used by the Pal. Tgs., the former by Ps.-Jon., the latter by Neof. All three expressions are mentioned in the following Mishnah: m. Git. IX:3 (also b. Git. 85a-b) "The essence of the *get* is in the words: 'Behold you are hereby permitted to any man.' R. Judah says: (He must add) and this shall be to you from me 'a writ of divorce' *sép̄er tērûkîn* = Tg. Ps.-Jon.), a 'letter of release' (*'iggéret šĕb̠ûqîn* = Tg. Neof.), and 'a bill of dismissal' (*gét pittûrîn* = Tg. Onq.), wherewith you may go and marry any man that you please."

who married her, dies, 4. the former husband who divorced her, is not permitted to remarry her, since she has been defiled, for that would be an abhorrence before the Lord; and you must not bring guilt upon the land, which the Lord your God is giving you for an inherited possession. 5. If a man had *recently married,*[2] he should not *be sent*[3] out to war nor have any assignment placed on him; he should be free for one year {to care} for his household, and bring happiness to the woman he has married. 6. Do not take millstones, not even the upper one, as a security pledge, because *with them food is produced for every person.*[4] 7. If a man is discovered to have kidnapped a fellow Israelite, then treating him as merchandise or selling him, that thief should *be put to death,*[5] and so you will remove *the evildoer*[6] from your midst. 8. Watch yourself very carefully in a case of the leprosy plague, to do according to all that the priests who are Levites instruct you to do; you should diligently observe what I have commanded them. 9. Remember what the Lord your God did to Miriam on the road after your departure from Egypt. 10. If you make any type of loan to your fellowman, do not go into his house to seize his security pledge. 11. You must stay outside, while the man to whom you made the loan brings the pledge out to you. 12. If he is a poor man, do not go to sleep with his security pledge {still in your possession}. 13. Be sure to return the security pledge at sunset, so that he may sleep with his clothes and bless you; and it will be to your merit before the Lord your God. 14. Do not take advantage of a hired laborer who is needy and destitute, whether he is one of your kinsmen or of your country's aliens {living} in your *city.*[7] 15. Pay him his wages on the same day and not after sunset, for he is needy and he is desperately counting on you; else he will cry out to the Lord against you and you will incur guilt. 16. Fathers will not die on account of the *testimony*[8] of the children, nor will children die on account of the *testimony*[8] of the fathers; each person dies for his own sin. 17. Do not pervert injustice in the case of an *alien*[a] or an orphan, nor take a widow's garment as a pledge. 18. Now you should remember that you were a slave *in*[b] Egypt, and the Lord your God redeemed you from there; therefore I command you to do this thing. 19. When you reap the harvest in your field and overlook a sheaf in the field, do not go back to retrieve it; leave it for the alien, for the orphan, and for the widow, in order that the Lord your God may bless you in all your undertakings. 20. When you shake your olives {from their trees}, do not bother with what is <left> behind you; leave it for the stranger, (for) the orphan, and (for) the widow. 21. When you glean your vineyard, do not harvest what is <left> behind you; leave it for the alien, (for) the orphan, and (for) the widow. 22. Now you should remember that you were a slave in the land of Egypt; therefore I command you to do this thing.

Apparatus, Chapter 24

[a] b, *d, and M have: "temporary resident."
[b] I adds: "the land of," as do some Hebrew mss., as well as some LXX mss. and Tg. Ps.-Jon.

Apparatus, Chapter 25

[a] g has: "judges."
[b] D has: "a stranger," as does the Hebrew.
[c] D, b, g, and i have: "refuses."

CHAPTER 25

1. When there is a dispute between men, and they approach the *court*[a] who renders a decision, acquitting the innocent and condemning the guilty, 2. if the guilty one *is sentenced*[1] to be flogged, the judge should place him in a lying down position and he should be given lashes in his presence, enough in number according to his guilt—3. forty lashes, no more, lest being flogged further in great excess, your brother be degraded in your eyes. 4. Do not muzzle *the mouth of*[2] an ox while it is threshing. 5. When brothers live together and one of them dies and leaves no *son,*[3] the wife of the dead one should not *marry*[4] *another man*[b] outside <the family>; her husband's brother should unite with her and take her as his wife, and fulfill the duty of a brother-in-law to her. 6. Now the first son that she will bear shall be accounted in *name*[5] to the dead brother, so that his name will not be blotted out from Israel. 7. But if the man does not want to marry his sister-in-law, his sister-in-law should go up to the gate *of the courthouse*[6] before the elders and declare, 'My husband's brother *does not wish*[c] to establish a name for his brother in Israel; he does not want to fulfill the duty of a brother-in-law towards me.'

Notes, Chapter 24 (Cont.)

[2]Lit. "taken a new wife."

[3]Lit. "go."

[4]The Hebrew has: "for that would be taking someone's life (or 'livelihood') as a security pledge." The Targum here expands on the Hebrew statement by explaining how, exactly, does this involve someone's life (or "livelihood")—since the millstones are used to produce food, which is essential for life. The Frg. Tg. (P, V) also paraphrases in this way, though adding further to it. This interpretive reading in the Targum is reflected in the following Mishnaic interpretation—m. B. Meṣ. IX:3 "... but everything with which we produce food for humans, as it is said: 'for he takes a man's life as pledge' (Deut. 24:6)."

[5]See above Chap. 17, n. 8, Chap. 18, n. 11, and Gen. Chap. 44, n. 6.

[6]See above Chap. 13, n. 7.

[7]See Gen. Chap. 22, n. 13.

[8]Lit. "mouth" paralleling the Rabbinic interpretation in the following texts:

1. *Sifre Kî Tēṣē'* CCLXXX, p. 297 "'The fathers should not be put to death on account of the children' (Deut. 24:16), but what does this verse come to teach us? That the fathers should not be put to death on account of the children, nor the children on account of the fathers? Has this not already been stated—'each one should be put to death on account of his own sin' (*ibid.*)? Rather (it means) that the fathers should not be put to death on the basis of the testimony of the sons, nor the sons on the basis of the testimony of the fathers." Cf. also b. Sanh. 27b, and y. Sanh. III:10, p. 21c, according to the latter the author of this interpretation is R. Aqiba. Cf. further A. Berliner, *Targum Onkelos: Einleitung...*, *op. cit.*, p. 243.

Notes, Chapter 25

[1]The idomatic Hebrew *bin* is here interpretively rendered to mean "is sentenced," lit. "is guilty," using *ḥayyab,* the same form used in the Syr., the Tgs. Ps.-Jon. and Neof. employing the *ithpa'al* form of the identical root. The Targum emphasizes that it is not merely enough for him to be "worthy" or "deserving" to be flogged, but he must be so sentenced in court.

[2]An insertion, also in Tg. Ps.-Jon., implied in the Hebrew.

[3]See Lev. Chap. 22, n. *e*.

[4]Lit. "be."

[5]This rendering is in direct opposition to the Halakha as stated in b. Yeb. 24a, where the *inheritance* rather than the *name* is to be understood.

[6]See above Chap. 21, n. 13.

8. Then the elders of the city should summon him and speak with him; if he insists, saying, 'I do not want to marry her,' 9. his sister-in-law should approach him in front of the elders and undo his sandal from his foot, and spit in his *presence*[7] saying, 'This is what should be done to the man who does not build up his brother's house. 10. His name in Israel should be known as 'The Family of the Unsandaled One.' 11. If two men get into a fight with one another and the wife of one approaches to save her husband from the assailant, and stretching out her hand she seizes him by his genitals. 12. *You should cut off her hand;*[8] show no mercy. 13. You should not have in your bag alternate weights, larger and smaller. 14. You should not have in your house alternate measures, a larger and a smaller. 15. You should have entirely honest weights and entirely honest measures, so that you may prolong your days in the land that the Lord your God is giving you. 16. For whosoever does these things, whoever deals deceitfully, is *abhorrent before*[d] the Lord your God. 17. Remember what Amalek did to you on the road after your departure from Egypt. 18. How he met you on the road and killed all the stragglers in your rear, when you were weary and worn out, and showed no reverence *from before*[9] *the Lord.*[e] 19. Therefore, when the Lord your God will grant you rest from all your enemies around you, in the land that the Lord your God is giving you as an inherited possession, you should erase the memory of Amalek from beneath the heaven; do not forget!

CHAPTER 26

1. When you will enter the land that the Lord your God is giving you as an inheritance, and take possession of it, then settle in it, 2. you should take some of every first fruit of the soil that you will *bring in*[a] from your land, that the Lord your God is giving you, and put <it> in a basket; then go to the place where the Lord your God will choose to make His *Shekhinah*[1] dwell. 3. Then you should go to the priest who will be <in residence> at the time, and say to him, 'I acknowledge this day *before*[2] the Lord your God, that I have entered the land that the Lord swore to our ancestors to give to us.' 4. Whereupon the priest should take the basket from your hand and *set it down*[b] in front of the altar of the Lord your God. 5. In response, you should then recite before the Lord your God, '*Laban the Aramaean sought to destroy my ancestor,*[3] who went down

Apparatus, Chapter 25 (Cont.)

[d] D has: "an abhorrence of," as does the Hebrew.

[e] D has: "of the Lord's *Yeqārā'*."

Apparatus, Chapter 26

[a] D has: "bring," using the root *'ty* instead of *'ll*.
[b] D, b, and g have: "deposited it," using *ṣn'* in place of *nḥt*.

[c] I has the plural, as does the LXX, as in 4:34 above.
[d] I has: "brought us in," using *'ll* instead of *'ty*.
[e] D has: "deposited it," for which cf. note *b* above.

to Egypt and lived there as a small nation; but eventually became a great, powerful, and populous nation there. 6. But the Egyptians dealt harshly with us, and imposed hard labor on us. 7. So we *prayed*[4] *before*[2] the Lord God of our fathers, and the Lord *accepted our prayer,*[5] as our plight, and our toil, as well as our oppression *were revealed before Him.*[6] 8. Then the Lord brought us out of Egypt with a powerful hand and a raised arm, with *a great manifestation,*[c] as well as with signs and (with) wonders. 9. Thereafter He *brought us*[d] to this place and gave us this land, a land *producing*[7] milk and honey. 10. So now, here I have brought the firstfruit of the soil that You, O Lord, have given me'; then you should *set it down*[e] before the Lord your God, and bow down

Notes, Chapter 25 (Cont.)

[7]The Targum here renders Hebrew *běp̱ānāw* "in his presence" by the term *bě'appôhî,* which here is a literal translation rather than to be understood as "into his face" in agreement with the Rabbinic interpretation here:

1. Sifre *Ki Tēṣē'* CCXCI, p. 310 "'and she should spit before him' (Deut. 25:9), I would think literally 'into his face,' it therefore says (*ibid.*) 'in sight of the elders,' spit that is visible to the elders."

2. b. Yeb. 106b "says Raba—the judges have to see when the spit emerges from the mouth of the brother's wife as it is written 'in sight of the elders and she should spit' (Deut. 25:9)."

[8]The Targum translates in accordance with the first opinion in Sifre (*ibid.* CCXCIII, p. 312) in opposition to R. Judah who interprets this phrase to mean "remuneration" rather than to be understood literally.

[9]See Gen. Chap. 4, n. 1.

Notes, Chapter 26

[1]Introduction VII D. 3.

[2]See Gen. Chap. 4, n. 1.

[3]The Hebrew *'ărammî 'ōḇēd 'āḇî* is sometimes rendered "my father was a wandering Aramaean" with "my father" as subject and "a wandering Aramaean" as a predicate adjective clause (so the NIV and RSV, and essentially the current JPS, only it substitutes "fugitive" for "wandering"). Others (ICC, the earlier JPS) have: "An Aramaean (the JPS has "Syrian") ready to perish was my father." Here, too, "my father" is still the subject, with *'ōḇēd* meaning "ready to perish" and to be understood as a relative clause modifying "Aramaean," still the predicate adjective. The Targum, however, makes "Aramaean" the subject, adds Laban to it, as that was his full name (Gen. 31:20). The term *'ōḇēd* is here made into a finite verb—"destroy," placed into the infinitive with the preceding verb "sought," and "my father" then becomes the direct object of the verb. This is essentially the approach also taken by Tg. Ps.-Jon.—"To Aram on the Rivers did our ancestor Jacob go down at the beginning, where he (= Laban) sought to destroy him," and by Tg. Neof.—"Laban the Aramaean sought to destroy our father Jacob from the beginning." Thus according to the Hebrew *'ōḇēd* refers to Jacob (whether it means "wandering," according to the later English versions, or "perish," according to the earlier versions), whereas the Targumim take *'ōḇēd* to refer to Laban with the meaning "cause to perish," i.e., "to destroy." The Sifre (*Kî Tāḇō'* CCCI, p. 319), however, contains an exposition of this phrase which applies *'ōḇēd* to both Jacob and Laban:
"'Now you should recite before the Lord your God *'ărammî 'ōḇēd 'āḇî*, teaching that Jacob only went down to Aram to disappear (*l'bd*) but it was attributed to Laban the Aramaean as if he destroyed him (*'ybdw*)." Thus we have here in this Midrash a play on the word *'bd*.

Cf. likewise *Midrash Tannaim to Deuteronomy* (ed. D.H. Hoffmann. Berlin, 1909, p. 172) which is even closer to the Targum than the above-cited Sifre—"Laban the Aramaean sought to destroy my ancestor, teaching that Jacob our ancestor only went down to Aram to disappear from the world, but it was attributed to Laban the Aramaean as if he destroyed him."

[4]See Exod. Chap. 8, n. 4.

[5]See Gen. Chap. 16, n. 1 and n. 5.

[6]See Gen. Chap. 29, n. 8.

[7]See Exod. Chap. 3, n. 12.

before the Lord your God. 11. Now you should rejoice for all the good things that the Lord your God has given to you and the members of your household, you, and the Levite, as well as the alien in your midst. 12. When you have finished setting aside a tenth of all your tithable produce in the third year, the year of the tithe, you should give it to the Levite, (to) the alien, (to) the orphan, and (to) the widow, so that they may eat to their satisfaction in your cities. 13. Then you should declare before the Lord your God, 'I have removed *the consecrated tithe*[f8] from the house, and, moreover, I have given it to the Levite and (to) the alien, as well as (to) the orphan, and (to) the stranger, according to all your commandments that you have issued me; I have neither transgressed nor neglected any of Your commandments. 14. I have not eaten of it while I was in mourning, nor have I *exchanged*[g] any of it for something defiled, nor have I deposited any of it with the dead; I have *listened to the Memra*[9] of the Lord my God; I have done according to all that You have commanded me. 15. Look down from Your sacred abode, from heaven and bless Your people Israel, and the land that You have given to us, as You swore to our ancestors—a land *producing*[7] milk and honey.' 16. The Lord your God commands you this day to follow these ordinances and laws, and diligently observe then with your entire heart and your entire soul. 17. You have *selected*[10] the Lord this day to be your God, and for you *to follow the paths that are proper before Him,*[11] as well as to observe His ordinances, His commandments, and His laws, and *to listen to His Memra.*[9] 18. And the Lord has *selected*[10] you this day to be His *beloved*[12] people as He has promised you and to observe all His commandments. 19. And that He will set you in praise, in fame, and in greatness over all the nations, for you to be a sacred nation before the Lord your God as He promised."

CHAPTER 27

1. Then Moses and the elders of Israel commanded the people as follows, "Observe all of the precept that I command you this day. 2. Moreover, on the day that you have crossed the Jordan to the land that the Lord your God is giving you, you should set up large stones and coat them with plaster. 3. Then inscribe upon them all the words of this

Apparatus, Chapter 26 (Cont.)

[f] Y_b, b, c, and g have: "the tithe belonging to the Sanctuary."

[g] D and h have: "remove." The rendering "exchanged," however, is reflected in Sifre (*Kî Tāḇō'* CCCIII, p. 322): "... Said R. Aqiba to him: If for a dead person (it is forbidden), it is (certainly) also forbidden for a living person, then why does it say 'for a dead person' (Deut. 26:14)? (To teach) that I did not *exchange* it even for something ritually permissible."

Apparatus, Chapter 27

[a] G has: "to," as does the Hebrew.

[b] I has: "those who curse."

[c] M has: "man," as does the Hebrew.

[d] D has: "an abhorrence of," as does the Hebrew.

law when you have crossed over to enter the land that the Lord your God is giving you—a land *producing*[1] milk and honey, as the Lord the God of your ancestors has *promised*[2] you. 4. And when you have crossed the Jordan, you should set up these stones on Mount Ebal and coat them with plaster as I command you this day. 5. Then you should build there an altar *before*[3] the Lord your God, an altar of stones; do not wield an iron <tool> over them. 6. You should build the altar of the Lord your God of whole stones, and offer upon it burnt offerings *before*[3] the Lord your God. 7. Then you should slaughter *sanctified sacrifices*[4] and eat them there, and rejoice before the Lord your God. 8. And you should inscribe very distinctly all the words of this law." 9. Then Moses and the priests who were Levites spoke *with*[a] all the Israelites, saying, "Listen, and hear, O Israel—This day you have become a people *before*[3] the Lord your God. 10. Now you should *listen to the Memra of*[5] the Lord your God and carry out all His commandments and His decrees, that I command you this day." 11. Then Moses commanded the people that day as follows, 12. "These {tribes} should stand on Mount Gerizim to bless the people after you have crossed the Jordan: Simeon, Levi, Judah, Issakhar, Joseph, and Benjamin. 13. These {tribes} should stand on Mount Ebal <to preside> over *the curses:*[b] Reuben, Gad, Asher, Zebulun, Dan, and Naphtali." 14. Then the Levites should respond by saying to every Israelite *person*[c] in a loud voice, 15. "Cursed be the man who makes a sculptured or molten image *abhorrent before*[d] the

Notes, Chapter 26 (Cont.)

[8]The Hebrew has the general term "consecrated matter," which the Targum specifies to mean the "tithes," mentioned in the preceding verse. The Midrash, likewise, spells it out to refer to the tithes as seen from Sifre (*ibid.* CCCIII, p. 321) "'I removed the consecrated matter from the house' (Deut. 26:13). This refers to the Second Tithe and the Fruits of the Fourth Year."

[9]See Gen. Chap. 22, n. 14.

[10]The Hebrew, a *hiphil* of the verb *'mr* "to say," is difficult here, and interpretively rendered to mean "select"—*ḥṭb*. The Tg. Ps.-Jon. likewise employs this identical root but elaborates: "You have selected (*ḥṭb*) the Lord as a unique entity *ḥṭybh* in the world this day (vs. 17) . . . and the Memra of the Lord has selected (*ḥṭb*) you as a unique entity *ḥṭybh* in the world this day" (vs. 18). The use of the root *ḥṭb* here is in complete agreement with Rabbinic interpretation of these passages by R. Eleazar b. Azariah as seen in the following texts:

b. Ḥag. 3a and *b. Ber.* 6a "Does, then, the Holy One, blessed be He, sing the praises of Israel?—Yes, for it is written: 'You have affirmed the Lord this day (Deut. 26:17) . . . and the Lord has avouched you this day' (*ibid.*, 18). The Holy One, blessed be He, said to Israel: You have made Me a unique entity (*ḥṭybh*) in the world, and I shall make you a unique entity (*ḥṭybh*) in the world . . . ."

Cf. also the Midrash Num. Rab. XIV:4 where the same exposition is contained. CTgD renders *'amleḵ* [*l'lykwnl*]—"considered you." F. Rosenthal (*Beth Talmud* 2 [1882]:280) thinks that *ḥṭb* is a Persian loanword meaning to consider, which makes sense according to CTgD cited above which has *'mlk* < *mlk*—"consider."

[11]See Gen. Chap. 18, n. 8.

[12]See Exod. Chap. 19, n. 5.

Notes, Chapter 27

[1]See Exod. Chap. 3, n. 13.

[2]Lit. "spoken to."

[3]See Gen. Chap. 4, n. 1.

[4]See Exod. Chap. 10, n. 11.

[5]See Gen. Chap. 22, n. 14.

Lord, the handiwork of a craftsman, and sets it up secretly; whereupon all the people should respond by saying, 'Amen.' 16. Cursed be he who disgraces his father or his mother; whereupon all the people should say, 'Amen.' 17. Cursed be he who moves his neighbor's landmark; whereupon all the people should say, 'Amen.' 18. Cursed be he who misdirects a blind person on the road; whereupon all the people should say, 'Amen.' 19. Cursed be he who perverts justice of the *alien,*[e] (of) the orphan, and (of) the widow; whereupon all the people should say, 'Amen.' 20. Cursed be he who lies with his father's wife, for he has revealed his father's *shame;*[6] whereupon all the people should say, 'Amen.' 21. Cursed be he who lies with any animal; whereupon all the people should say, 'Amen.' 22. Cursed be he who lies with his sister, the daughter of his father or the daughter of his mother; whereupon all the people should say, 'Amen.' 23. Cursed be he who lies with his mother-in-law; whereupon all the people should say, 'Amen.' 24. Cursed be he who *strikes down*[f] his neighbor secretly; whereupon all the people should say, 'Amen.' 25. Cursed be he who *accepts*[7] a bribe to kill an innocent person; whereupon all the people should say, 'Amen.' 26. Cursed be he who does not uphold the words of this law to observe them; whereupon all the people should say, 'Amen.'

CHAPTER 28

1. Now if you will completely *accept the Memra of*[1] the Lord your God, to diligently observe all His commandments which I issue you this day, the Lord your God will set you over all the nations of the earth. 2. Then all these blessings will come upon you, and overtake you because you *accepted the Memra of*[1] the Lord your God. 3. Blessed shall you be in the city, and blessed shall you be in the field. 4. Blessed shall be the *child*[2] of your womb and the fruit of your soil, the offspring of your cattle, the calves of your herd and the lambs of your flock. 5. Blessed shall be your basket and your kneading trough. 6. Blessed shall you be in your comings, and blessed shall you be in your goings. 7. The Lord will cause your enemies who rise up against you to be *shattered*[3] before you; they will march out on one road towards you, but they will flee from before you on seven roads. 8. The Lord will assign *for*[a] you blessing to your storehouses and to all your undertakings, and He will bless you in the land that the Lord your God is giving you. 9. The Lord will establish you *before*[b] Him as a sacred people as

Apparatus, Chapter 27 (Cont.)

[e] M has: "the temporary resident."

[f] I has: "kills."

Apparatus, Chapter 28

[a] D, b, *d, and g have: "with," as does the Hebrew.

[b] D, b, and g have: "for," as does the Hebrew.

[c] b, *d, and g, as well as M, have: "provoke against."

[d] D and b have: "it has destroyed you," as does the Hebrew. Some Sam. Heb. mss. have: "they have destroyed you" as they do in vs. 20 above.

He swore to you, if you will observe the commandments of the Lord your God *and follow the paths that are proper before Him.*[4] 10. Then all the nations of the earth will realize that the name of the Lord is proclaimed over you, and they will fear you. 11. Moreover, the Lord will grant you abundant prosperity with regard to the *child*[2] of your womb, and the offspring of your cattle, as well as the fruit of your soil, in the land that He swore to your ancestors to give you. 12. The Lord will open up to you His prosperous storehouse—the heavens—to provide rain in its {proper} season for your land, and to bless all your undertakings; you will lend to many nations but borrow from none. 13. Then the Lord will make you *strong, not weak,*[5] and you will only be at the top, not on the bottom, because you *accepted*[6] the commandments of the Lord your God that I issue you this day, to diligently observe. 14. Moreover, you should not deviate to the right or to the left from any of the *commandments*[7] that I issue you this day to follow the *idols of other nations*[8] in worshipping them. 15. But if you will not *accept the Memra of*[1] the Lord your God to diligently observe all His commandments and His ordinances that I command you this day, then all these curses will come upon you and overtake you. 16. Cursed shall you be in the city and cursed shall you be in the field. 17. Cursed shall be your basket and your kneading trough. 18. Cursed shall be the *child*[2] of your womb and the fruit of your soil, the calves of your herd and the lambs of your flock. 19. Cursed shall you be in your comings, and cursed shall you be in your goings. 20. May the Lord *send on*[c] you calamity, chaos, and rebuke in all your undertakings in which you engage, until you are destroyed and summarily ruined on account of the evil of your deeds *in your abandonment of My reverence.*[9] 21. May the Lord make pestilence cling to you, until it will cut you off from the land that you are entering to take possession of it. 22. May the Lord strike you with consumption, fever, and inflammation, with scorching heat and drought, with blight and mildew; and let them hound you until you will perish. 23. Now the skies above your head will be *as hard as*[10] copper *in withholding rain,*[10] and the earth below you *as obstinate as*[10] iron *in not producing fruit.*[10] 24. May the Lord turn the rain of your land into dust and powder; may it then come down on you from the skies until *you are destroyed.*[d] 25. May the Lord cause you to be *shattered*[3] before your enemy; you will march out to him by a single road and flee from him by seven roads; moreover, you will become a horror to all

Notes, Chapter 27 (Cont.)

[6]See above Chap. 23, n. 1.
[7]See Gen. Chap. 4, n. 8.

Notes, Chapter 28

[1]See Gen. Chap. 22, n. 14.
[2]See Gen. Chap. 3, n. 8.
[3]See Lev. Chap. 26, n. 16.
[4]See Gen. Chap. 18, n. 8.
[5]The Hebrew: "the head, not the tail" is a figure of speech and accordingly rendered into the intended meaning. Similarly below in vs. 44—"he will be the head and you the tail."
[6]See Gen. Chap. 16, n. 1.
[7]Lit. "words" or "matters," or "things."
[8]See Introduction VII A.3.
[9]See Introduction VII B.3.
[10]See Lev. Chap. 26, n. 17.

the kingdoms of the earth. 26. Now your carcass will become food for every bird of the sky and all the beasts of the earth; and there will be no one to drive them away. 27. May the Lord strike you with the *boils of Egypt*[e] and with hemorrhoids, boil-scars, and the dry itch, from which you cannot be cured. 28. May the Lord strike you with madness, blindness, and stupefaction. 29. Now you will be groping at noon as a blind man gropes in the dark, and you will not prosper in *your ways;*[f] all you will ever be is constantly oppressed and robbed with no one to rescue you. 30. You will become betrothed to a woman, but another man *will lie with her;*[11] you will build a house, but you will not live in it; you will plant a vineyard, but you will not make general use of it. 31. Your ox will be slaughtered before your eyes, but you will not eat of it; your donkey will be seized in front of you, but it will not be returned to you; your flock will be delivered to your enemies, with no one to help you. 32. Your sons and daughters will be delivered to another nation, and your eyes will be strained from watching for them every day; and you will be powerless. 33. A people you do not know will eat the fruit of your soil, as well as everything your labor <produced>; and you will be continually oppressed and downtrodden. 34. Then you will become insane from the sights your eyes will behold. 35. May the Lord afflict you with severe boils on your knees and (on the) thighs, from which you cannot be cured; from the sole of your foot to your brain. 36. May the Lord *exile*[12] you, and your king whom you will establish over you, to a nation which you do not know—<not> you nor your ancestors—and there you will labor for nations who worship *idols*[8] of wood and stone. 37. You will be a consternation, a proverb, and a byword, among all the nations where the Lord will *lead*[g] you. 38. Much seed will you take out *to*[13] the field, but you will gather in little, for the *locust*[h] will *consume it.*[i] 39. You will plant vineyards and till them; but you will drink no wine nor gather <the grapes> for the worm will devour it. 40. You will have olive trees throughout your territory; but you will not have any oil for anointment, for your olive shall drop off. 41. You will bear sons and daughters, but you will not have them with you, for they will go into captivity. 42. The locust will *take over*[j] all your trees and the fruit of your soil. 43. The *uncircumcised transient*[14] in your midst will rise above you higher and higher, while you will sink lower and lower. 44. He will lend to you, but you will not lend to him; he will be *strong,*[5] but you will be *weak.*[5] Now all these curses will happen to you

Apparatus, Chapter 28 (Cont.)

[e] D, b, and g have: "boils of the Egyptians."

[f] b, *d, g, and l have the singular, as does the Syr. and the Sam. Heb., as well as a number of Hebrew variants in Kennicott. D has: "the way of your goodness."

[g] D has: "exile," which is interpretive.

[h] The Arukh has the expected plural.

[i] l has: "take it over," as the Hebrew has in vs. 42 below.

[j] D has: "ruin," using the root *trk* instead of *ḥsn* for the Hebrew *yrš* applied here to the action of the locusts. The Sam. Heb. has the *hiphil* of *yrš* which is equivalent to Aramaic *trk*.

[k] D has: "it has destroyed you," as in vs. 24 above. The Sam. Heb., the Vetus Latina, and the Syr. have: "they have destroyed you."

[l] D has the plural in both cases, b and g only in the first.

[m] D has: "honesty."

[n] Using *šm‘*, the same root as the Hebrew, whereas i uses *yd‘* with the same meaning, and D has "accept" (*qbl*).

[o] D and b have: "it has destroyed you," as do the Hebrew, the Syr., the Sam. Heb., and a Hebrew variant in Kennicott, whereas the Vetus Latina has: "until they have destroyed you."

[p] c has: "cities."

[q] h omits, as does the LXX.

[r] c adds: "all" as do some LXX mss. and the Syr. The Hebrew has "all" at the end of vs. 55 above.

[s] i has: "great," which is the standard adjective in combination with the others listed here, for which see Deut. 10:17; Jer. 32:18; Dan. 9:4; and Neh. 1:5.

[t] D has: "numerous."

[u] D has: "misfortunes."

and haunt you and overtake you until *you are destroyed;*[k] because you did not *accept the Memra of*[1] the Lord your God, to observe His commandments and His ordinance which I commanded you. 46. They will be as *a sign*[1] and as *a wonder*[1] to you and your *descendents*[2] forever. 47. Precisely because you did not worship *before*[15] the Lord your God, with joy and with *goodness*[m] of heart over the abundance of everything. 48. Then you will serve, in hunger and in thirst, in nakedness and in lacking all, your enemies whom the Lord has incited against you, and He will put an iron yoke upon Your neck until He has destroyed you. 49. May the Lord bring against you a nation from afar, from the ends of the earth as the eagle swings down, a people whose language you do not *understand.*[n] 50. A nation, ruthless, which does not have respect for the elderly nor *mercy*[16] for the young. 51. Now it will consume the *offspring*[2] of your beasts and the fruit of your soil until *you are destroyed,*[o] that you will not have left any grain, wine, or oil, calves of your herd, and the lambs of your flock, until it ruins you. 52. He will lay siege to you in all your *cities,*[17] until it will have overcome the high and fortified walls which you trusted to be saved through them throughout your *land;*[p] and he will lay siege to you *in all your cities*[q17] throughout your entire land, which the Lord your God is giving you. 53. Now you will eat the *child*[2] of your womb—the flesh of your own sons and daughters that the Lord your God has given you, because of the narrow straits that your enemy has pressed you. 54. The most tender and fastidious person among you will act meanly towards his brother, towards *the wife of his covenant,*[18] and towards his remaining children who are left, 55. from giving to any of them any of the flesh of {those of} his children that he eats, because nothing else remained for him, on account of the narrow straits into which your enemy has pressed you. 56. The one who is most tender and fastidious among you, who has not even ventured to set foot on the ground because of tenderness and fastidiousness, will act meanly towards *the husband of her covenant*[18] and (towards) her son and (towards) her daughter, 57. and towards the *youngest of her children that emerges from her,*[19] as well as towards the children that she bore; she will eat them secretly because of desperate need, on account of the narrow straits into which your enemies have pressed you *in*[r] your *cities.*[17] 58. If you will not diligently observe all the terms of this law that are inscribed in this document, to revere this *honored*[s] and awesome Name, the Lord your God, 59. then the Lord will make your plagues and the plagues against your *descendants,*[2]*exceptional*[t] ones and lasting *plagues,*[u] as well as severe and lasting diseases. 60. Moreover, He will bring back on you all the afflictions of

Notes, Chapter 28 (Cont.)

[11]The Hebrew *kĕtîb* has: "will ravish (*šgl*) her, "whereas the *qĕrê* is "lie with her" *škb*, here followed by the Targum and the Sam. Tg.

[12]The Hebrew has the general term—"lead" or "bring," which the Targum (as well as Tgs. Ps.-Jon. and Neof.) renders interpretively by the specific term "exile."

[13]An insertion implied in the Hebrew.

[14]See Lev. Chap. 25, n. 10.

[15]See Gen. Chap. 4, n. 1.

[16]See Gen. Chap. 6, n. 8.

[17]See Gen. Chap. 22, n. 13.

[18]See above Chap. 13, n. 8.

[19]The Hebrew has the very descriptive: "the afterbirth that emerges from between her legs" which the Targum here renders euphemistically.

Egypt[v] which you dreaded, and they will cling to you. 61. Also *every misfortune and plague*[w] which are not inscribed in this document of the Law will the Lord bring on you, until *you are destroyed.*[x] 62. Now you will be left a small nation after having been as numerous as the stars in heaven, because you did not *accept the Memra of*[1] the Lord your God. 63. And as the Lord once delighted in making you prosperous and (making you) numerous, so will the Lord delight in ruining you and destroying you; and you will be removed from the land which you are entering to take possession of it. 64. Then the Lord will scatter you among all the nations from one end of the earth to the other end of the earth; and there you will serve nations who worship *idols,*[8] whom you or your ancestors had never known, {idols} of wood and stone. 65. Yet even among *these*[y] nations you will not have tranquility, nor will the sole of your foot find a place to rest; and there the Lord will give you an anguished heart, dimness of sight, and a despondent spirit. 66. Moreover, you will live in constant suspense and be in a state of anxiety by night and by day, never sure of your life. 67. In the morning you will say, 'I wish it were evening'; and in the evening you will say, 'I wish it were morning'; because of the inner anxiety that you will experience and because of the sights that your eyes will see. 68. Then the Lord will return you to Egypt in ships by a route I told you that you should never see it again; and there you will be offered up for sale to your enemies as male and female slaves, but none will buy. 69. These are the terms of the covenant that the Lord commanded Moses to establish *with*[z] the Israelites in the land of Moab; in addition to the covenant that He established with them at Ḥoreb."

CHAPTER 29

1. Then Moses summoned all of *Israel*[a] and said to them, "You have seen all that the Lord had done before your very eyes in the land of Egypt, to the Pharaoh and to his officials, as well as to his land. 2. The great miracles which your eyes saw, these great signs and wonders. 3. But to this day the Lord has not given you a heart to understand

Apparatus, Chapter 28 (Cont.)

[v] M and c have: "the Egyptians."
[w] D has: "all misfortunes and all plagues."
[x] D, c, and b have: "it has destroyed you," as does a Hebrew variant in Kennicott, the Syr., and the Vg.
[y] D and c have: "these."
[z] Understanding Hebrew *'t* as the preposition "with," whereas D omits it, understanding *'t* as the accusative particle and rendering it *yt*.

Apparatus, Chapter 29

[a] I has: "the Israelites," while s has: "the elders of Israel."
[b] D adds: "neither."
[c] D has: "tear" as in Deut. 8:4 above.
[d] D has: "intoxicating drink."
[e] M has: "conquered," which is interpretive.
[f] I has: "to," as does the Hebrew.
[g] c and d omit.
[h] So also T, j, and i, whereas Sperber's main text has: "among whom you dwell."
[i] b has the interpretive: "straying."
[j] So also Sperber's main text, thus translating only the Hebrew *l'bd* but omitting a translation for the preceding *llkt,* whereas, U, c, d, j, and i only translate *llkt* but not *l'bd.*

and[b] eyes to see, as well as ears to hear. 4. Moreover, I led you through the wilderness {for} forty years; your clothes did not wear out from your back; neither did your sandals *wear out*[c] on your feet. 5. You had no bread to eat nor any new wine or *old wine*[d] to drink; so that you might realize that I am the Lord your God. 6. Then you came to this territory; whereupon Siḥon, king of Ḥeshbon, and Og, king of *Maṯnan,*[1] marched out to meet you to *wage*[2] war, but we defeated them. 7. So we *took*[e] their land and gave it as an inherited possession to *the tribe of*[3] Reuben and to *the tribe of*[3] Gad, as well as to the half tribe of Manasseh. 8. Now you should observe the terms of this covenant and follow them, so that you will prosper in all that you will do. 9. You stand this day, all of you, before the Lord your God; your leaders, your tribal officials, your elders, and your commanders, every person of Israel, 10. your children, your wives, and your aliens who are within your camp, from the one who gathers your wood to the one who draws your water, 11. *to bring you into*[4] the covenant of the Lord your God and into His oath, which the Lord your God is establishing with you this day, 12. in order to confirm you this day as His people *before*[f] Him that He may be *your God*[5] as he *promised*[6] you, and as He swore to your ancestors—to Abraham, to Isaac, and to Jacob. 13. Not exclusively with you do I establish this covenant and this oath, 14. but with those that are standing here with us this day before the Lord our God, as well as with *those that are*[g] not with us here this day. 15. For you know how we lived in the land of Egypt and how we passed through the midst of *various*[7] nations *through whom you had to pass.*[h] 16. Then you saw their abominations, their idols of wood, and stone, of silver and gold among them. 17. Perchance there is among you a man or a woman or a family or a clan, whose heart even this day, is *turning*[i] away from *the reverence of*[8] the Lord your God *to worship*[j] *the idols of these nations;*[9] perchance there is among you *a man with sinful or presumptuous thoughts.*[10] 18. When he hears the words of this oath *he may think to himself*[11] as

Notes, Chapter 29

[1]See Num. Chap. 21, n. 23.

[2]See Num. Chap. 10, n. 1.

[3]See above Chap. 3, n. 5.

[4]The Hebrew *lĕʿoḇrĕḵā biḇrîṯ* denotes "entering into a covenant." According to Schefftel (*Bi'ure Onqelos, op. cit.*, p. 267) the root *ʿbr* in Aramaic in conjunction with "covenant" denotes just the reverse—"transgression of a covenant." Consequently, the Targum employs the *aphel* of *ʿll*—"to bring into" as if the Hebrew had *lahăḇîʾăkā* (*hiphil* of *bwʾ*). The combination *bwʾ* (*hiphil* or *qal*) together with *bĕrîṯ* occurs in Hebrew with precisely this very meaning—"to enter into a covenant," as Löwenstein (*Nefesh Ha-Ger, op. cit.*, p. 47) points out in 1 Sam. 20:8 and Jer. 34:10 which the Tg. Neb. renders identically to Tg. Onq. in the present verse. Tg. Ps.-Jon. employs the same term.

[5]Lit. "a God to you."

[6]Lit. "spoke to."

[7]Lit. "the."

[8]See Introduction VII B.3.

[9]See Introduction VII A.3.

[10]The Hebrew has: "a root sprouting poison weed and wormwood," which is a figure of speech. The Targum accordingly renders it into its intended meaning, with "root" symbolizing man who harbors the wrong thoughts (=Hebrew "sprouting poison weed and wormwood"). Tg. Neof. elaborates on this figure of speech indicating precisely the symbolism involved—"let there not be among you a man whose heart meditates on sin, since he is likened to a root fixed in the ground; for the beginning of sin is sweet as honey, but its end is bitter as wormwood of death."

[11]Lit. "he may think in his heart," which involves the rare Hebrew expression "he may bless himself in his heart," here rendered by the Targum interpretively to mean "think (erroneously) to himself." The other

follows, 'I will be safe, though I will follow the *thoughts of*[12] my heart,' *so that he adds unintentional transgressions to his presumptuous ones.*[13] 19. The Lord will not forgive him, rather the Lord's anger and passion will *intensify*[14] against that man, and all the curses that are inscribed in this document will *cleave*[15] to him, and the Lord will erase his name from beneath the heavens. 20. The Lord will single him out from all the tribes of Israel for disaster, according to all the curses of the covenant that are inscribed in this document of the Law. 21. Now a later generation—your children who succeed you and a *foreigner*[16] who will come from a distant land, who will see the plagues <that have afflicted> that land, and the misfortunes that the Lord has brought against it, 22. all its soil devastated by sulphur and salt, never to be sowed again nor to ever grow anything again; nor will there ever come up any grass on it, like the upheaval of Sodom and Gomorrah, Admah, and Zeboiim, which the Lord overthrew in His furious anger. 23. Now all the nations will *ask,*[17] 'Why has the Lord done this to this land? How intense is this great anger!' 24. Then they will *answer,*[17] 'Because they abandoned the covenant of the Lord, the God of their ancestors, which He established with them when He brought them out of the land of Egypt, 25. they proceeded to worship *the idols of the nations*[9] and bowed down to them, deities whom they did not know, and which could not do any good for them.' 26. Then the Lord's anger intensified against the land, so as to bring over it all the curses that are inscribed in this document. 27. Whereupon He removed them from their land in violent anger and with great fury, *exiling*[18] them to another land to this day. 28. Secret things belong to the Lord our God, whereas revealed things belong to us and to our children forever, to follow all the words of this Law.

CHAPTER 30

1. When all these things—the *blessings*[1] and the *curses*[1]—that I have set before you, will happen to you, and you take them to heart amidst the various nations where the Lord has exiled you, 2. and you return to the *reverence for*[2] the Lord your God and accept His Memra with your entire heart and your entire soul according to everything I command you this day, you and your children, 3. then the Lord your God in His compassion on you will reverse your *exile,*[a] and reassemble you from all the nations where the Lord your God scattered you. 4. Even if your banishment be at the ends of the heavens, from there the Lord your God will reassemble you, and from there He will *bring you near.*[b] 5. Then the Lord your God will bring you into the land that your ancestors inherited, and you shall inherit it and fare well; while He will favor you and make you more numerous than your ancestors. 6. Moreover, the Lord your God will

Apparatus, Chapter 30

[a] A, B, D, l, and i have: "captivity," as does the Hebrew.
[b] b and g have: "take you," as does the Hebrew.
[c] l adds: "the worship of."

remove the obduracy of[3] your heart *and the obduracy of*[3] the heart of your offspring; *so that you may*[4] *love*[c] the Lord your God with your entire heart and with your entire soul in order that you may live. 7. Then the Lord your God will direct all these curses against your enemies and (against your) adversaries who persecuted you. 8. Now you will again *accept the Memra of*[5] the Lord and observe all His commandments which I issue you this day. 9. Moreover, the Lord will grant you abounding prosperity in all your undertakings—in the *children*[6] of your womb, in the offspring of your cattle, and in the fruit of your soil; because the Lord will again rejoice in favoring you as He rejoiced in that of your ancestors. 10. Because you *accepted the Memra of*[5] the Lord your God to observe His commandments and His ordinances that are inscribed in this document of the Law; for you returned to *the reverence for*[2] the Lord your God with your entire heart and your entire soul. 11. For this precept that I issue you this day is not too removed from you, nor is it *beyond reach.*[7] 12. It is not in heaven as if to say, 'Who will go up to heaven for us and get it and proclaim it to us, that we may observe it?" 13. Nor is it beyond the sea as if to say, 'Who will cross the other side of the sea for us and get it for us

Notes, Chapter 29 (Cont.)

Aramaic versions also render this Hebrew expression interpretively—the Syr. and Sam. Tg. are identical to Tg. Onq. (the former even employing the same root—*ḥšb,* the latter *sbr*); Tg. Ps.-Jon. "he will be careless in his heart" (*y'š*), Tg. Neof. "he will pacify himself with the thoughts in his heart." The Vg. is literal here, while the LXX has: καὶ ἐπιφημίσηται ἐν τῇ καρδίᾳ αὐτοῦ—"he will flatter himself in his heart."

[12]The Hebrew *šryrwt* "uprightness," "honesty" is here rendered simply "thoughts," as the latter is usually associated with heart. The following Midrash reflects this interpretation—Eccl. Rab. 1:16 ". . . the heart 'thinks' or 'plans' or 'conceives' (*mhrhr,* employing the same root as the Targum does here), as it is said 'though I follow the imaginations of my heart' (Deut. 29:18)." Cf. also Num. 15:39 where the Hebrew has "hearts" and the Targum translates "the thoughts"; there the subject being man straying after the thoughts of his heart, which are innately evil (cf. Gen. 8:21). In fact Tg. Ps.-Jon. here has precisely the language of the Genesis passage (8:21) "for I will follow the power of the evil inclination that is in my heart." Tg. Neof. in contrast is totally literal here, having *qšytwt lyby*—"the uprightness of my heart."

[13]The Hebrew "to the utter ruin of the moist and the dry alike" is highly figurative, and accordingly paraphrased by the Targum into its intended meaning. Tgs. Ps.-Jon. and Neof. render similarly here. The Targum understood the Hebrew infinitive *spwt* here to be associated with the root *ysp* "add" instead of the root *sph* "destroy."

[14]The Hebrew "burn," "smoke" is figurative and accordingly rendered by its intended meaning. Tgs. Ps.-Jon. and Neof., as well as the Sam. Tg., employ the same term here.

[15]The Hebrew *rāḇṣāh* < *rbṣ* "lie," "crouch" is figurative and accordingly rendered by its intended meaning. Tg. Neof. renders similarly, while Tg. Ps.-Jon. has "effect him," and the Syr. simply "come on him."

[16]See Gen. Chap. 17, n. 7.

[17]Lit. "say."

[18]The Hebrew has: "I will cast them." The Targum paraphrases the Hebrew idiom to avoid imparting the concrete action of casting to God.

Notes, Chapter 30

[1]See Gen. Chap. 21, n. 7.

[2]See Introduction VII B.3.

[3]See above Chap. 10, n. 6.

[4]Lit. "in order to."

[5]See Gen. Chap. 22, n. 14.

[6]See Gen. Chap. 3, n. 8.

[7]Lit. "too far."

and proclaim it to us, that we may observe it?' 14. Rather the matter is very close to you, in your mouth, and in your heart, to observe it. 15. Realize I set before you this day life and prosperity, death, and disaster. 16. In that I command you this day to *love*[c] the Lord your God, *to follow the paths that are proper before*[d] *Him,*[8] and to observe His commandments, and His ordinances, as well as His laws; then you will survive and increase, and the Lord your God will bless you in the land which you are about to enter and possess. 17. But if your heart turns away and does not *listen,*[9] and you are led astray into bowing down to *the idols of the nations*[10] and to worship them, 18. I inform you this day that you will surely perish; you will not endure in the land which you are crossing the Jordan to enter and possess. 19. This day I call heaven and earth as witnesses against you; I have set before you life and death, *blessings*[1] and *curses;*[1] now you should choose life so that you and your *children*[6] may live, 20. by *loving*[c] the Lord your God, *by accepting His Memra*[5] *and by staying close to His reverence;*[11] for He is your life and the *one who prolongs*[12] your days, to endure in the land that the Lord swore to your ancestors to Abraham, to Isaac, and to Jacob, to give to them."

CHAPTER 31

1. Then Moses proceeded to speak these words to all of Israel. 2. Now he said to them, "I am a hundred and twenty years old this day; I am no longer able to come and go; and the Lord said to me, 'You may not cross this Jordan.' 3. The Lord your God, it is *He*[a] who will cross at your head, He will destroy these nations before you and dispossess them; Joshua is the one who will cross at your head, as the Lord has spoken. 4. Moreover, the Lord will do to them as He did to Siḥon and Og, the Amorite kings and to their land, in that He destroyed them. 5. Then the Lord will deliver them before you, and you will do to them in complete compliance with the command that I issue you. 6. Be strong and courageous, do not be afraid nor be in dread on account of them; for the Lord your God—*His Memra*[b] will march at your head; He will not abandon you nor *will He be far away from you.*[1]" 7. Then Moses summoned Joshua and said to him in sight of all of Israel, "Be strong and courageous, for you will *enter with this*[c] people into the land that I swore to their ancestors to give to them; and you will allot it to them

Apparatus, Chapter 30

[d] I has: "to."

Apparatus, Chapter 31

[a] I has: "His Memra."

[b] I has: "He," as does the Hebrew.

[c] b and *d have: "bring this," understanding Hebrew אֵת here as the accusative particle instead of the preposition, as in vs. 23 below. For a discussion of the difficulty in the Hebrew dealing with the Ancient Versions, see B. Grossfeld, "Targum Neofiti I to Deut. 31:7," *JBL* 91 (1972):533-4; and *idem.*, "Neofiti I to Deut. 31:7—The Problem Re-Analyzed," *ABR* 24 (1976):30-34.

[d] G has: "on that day," as does the Hebrew, while b and g have it for the second occurrence in this verse and vs. 18 below.

as an inherited possession. 8. Whereas the Lord, He will march at your head, *His Memra will be your support,*[2] He will not abandon you, nor *will He be far away from you.*[1]" 9. Then Moses wrote down this Law and gave it to the priests, the descendants of Levi, who carried the Ark of the Lord's Covenant, and to the elders of Israel. 10. Moreover, Moses commanded them as follows, "At the end of seven years, at the period of the year of remission, during the Festival of Booths, 11. when all of Israel comes to appear before the Lord your God, in the place which He will choose, you should read this Law before all of Israel *and make them hear it.*[3] 12. Assemble the people—men, women, and children, as well as the alien in your cities, in order that they may hear and in order that they may learn to act in reverence *before*[4] the Lord your God, and diligently observe all the words of this Law. 13. Even their children who are not yet knowledgeable, should hear and learn to act reverentially *before*[4] the Lord your God, all the time that you are in existence in the land which you are about to cross the Jordan to possess." 14. Then the Lord said to Moses, "Here, the day of your death is approaching; summon Joshua and present yourselves at the Tent of Meeting where I will commission him"; so Moses and Joshua went and presented themselves at the Tent of Meeting. 15. Whereupon the Lord *revealed Himself*[5] in the Tent in a pillar of cloud, the pillar of cloud hovering over the entrance of the Tent. 16. Then the Lord said to Moses, "Here, you are about to lie with your ancestors, and this people will thereupon proceed to stray after *the idols of the nations*[6] of the land which you are about to enter into their midst and they will abandon *My reverence*[7] and *alter*[8] My covenant that I established with *them.*[9] 17. Thereupon My anger will intensify against *them,*[9] *at that time,*[d] and *I will keep them at a distance from Me*[1] *and remove My Shekhinah*[10] from

Apparatus, Chapter 31 (Cont.)

[8]See Gen. Chap. 18, n. 8.
[9]See Gen. Chap. 16, n. 1.
[10]See Introduction VII A.3.
[11]See above Chap. 10, n. 10.
[12]Lit. "length of."

Notes, Chapter 31

[1]The Hebrew has: "forsake" which one would have expected the Targum to render literally by the root *šbq*. However, in view of the fact that he already used it for the preceding verb, he avoids duplication by employing *rḥq*—"to be far away," in a similar sense. The same technique was employed by Tg. Ps.-Jon. In contrast, Tg. Neof., the Sam. Tg., and the Syr. all of whom rendering the preceding Hebrew verb literally by the indentical root (*rph-rpy*), employ *šbq* in this case.

[2]See Gen. Chap. 26, n. 2.

[3]The Hebrew figure of speech "into their ears" is here paraphrased into its intended meaning.

[4]See Gen. Chap. 4, n. 1.

[5]See Gen. Chap. 12, n. 5.

[6]See Introduction VII A.3.

[7]See Introduction VII B.3.

[8]See Lev. Chap. 26, n. 14.

[9]Starting from this point in vs. 16 through vs. 21 (with three exceptions in vs. 17) the Targum, as well as Tgs. Neof. and Ps.-Jon., the LXX, and the Sam. Heb. pluralize the singular pronoun of the Hebrew referring back to the people. The exceptions in vs. 17 "*it* will say," "in *my* midst," and "happened to *me*" are only in Tg. Onq.; the two Pal. Tgs. have the plural here as well.

[10]The anthropomorphism of the Hebrew "and hide My face" is here circumvented by the use of *Shekhinah* for which cf. Introduction VII D.3.

them, leaving *them*[9] open to be *plundered;*[e] whereupon numerous misfortunes and distressing situations will happen to *them,*[9] and it will be said *at that time.*[d] Indeed, because *the Shekhinah of*[11] my God is not in my midst did these misfortunes happen to me. 18. Now I will surely *remove My Shekhinah*[10] *from them*[12] *at that time*[d] for all the evil that *they*[f9] committed in that *they*[9] followed *the idols of the nations.*[6] 19. So now, write down this song of praise and teach it to the Israelites; put it in their mouths, in order that this song of praise should be a witness *before*[g] Me against the Israelites. 20. When I will bring *them*[9] into the land that I promised on oath to *their*[9] ancestors, one *producing*[13] milk and honey, and *they*[9] will eat to *their*[9] satisfaction and delight, and then follow *the idols of the nations*[6] and worship them, *causing provocation before Me*[14] and *altering*[8] My covenant, 21. and when numerous misfortunes and distressing situations will happen to *them,*[9] this song of praise will act as a respondent *before*[4] Him as a witness, since it will not be forgotten from the mouths of *their*[9] *descendants,*[15] because *their*[9] thoughts which *they are*[h9] planning to carry out *are revealed before Me*[16] this day, before I bring *them*[9] into the land that I promised on oath." 22. So Moses wrote down this song of praise that day and taught it to the Israelites. 23. Then he commanded Joshua, son of Nun, saying, "Be strong and courageous for you are about to bring the Israelites into the land that I promised them on oath, and *My Memra will be your support.*[2]" 24. When Moses concluded to write down the words of this Law into a document to their very end, 25. Moses commanded the Levites, the carriers of the Ark of the Lord's covenant as follows, 26. "*Take*[i] this document of the Law and place it beside the Ark of the Covenant of the Lord your God, where it should be as a witness against you. 27. Well do I know your rebelliousness and stubbornness; here, even as I am still alive in your midst this day, you are rebellious *before*[4] the Lord; how much more so after I die! 28. Gather to me all the elders of your tribes and your officials, so that I may *speak*[j] these words *before them*[k17] and call heaven and earth as witness against *them.*[l] 29. Well do I know that after I die you will surely become corrupt and deviate from the path that I commanded you, and misfortune will happen to you at the end of days; for you will commit that which is evil *before*[4] the Lord *to cause provocation before Him*[14] by your deeds." 30. Then Moses spoke the words of this song of praise in the presence of the entire community of Israel until their very end.

Apparatus, Chapter 31 (Cont.)

[e] g and l have: "consumed," as does the Hebrew.

[f] k and l have: "he," as does the Hebrew, whereas Tgs. Ps.-Jon. and Neof., the Sam. Heb., one LXX ms., and the Sebirin have: "they."

[g] A has: "for," as does the Hebrew.

[h] d_a has: "it (= the people) is," as does the Hebrew.

[i] I has the interpretive: "accept."

[j] j adds: "all," as does a variant in Kennicott, and Tg. Ps.-Jon.

[k] c and s have: "you" (masc. pl.).

[l] So also T and i, whereas Sperber's main text has: "you" (masc. pl.)

Notes, Chapter 30 (Cont.)

[11]For this insertion, see Introduction VII D.3.

[12]An insertion influenced by its presence in the Hebrew of the preceding verse.

[13]See Exod. Chap. 3, n. 12.

[14]See Num. Chap. 14, n. 8.

[15]See Gen. Chap. 3, n. 8.

[16]See Gen. Chap. 3, n. 1.

[17]See Gen. Chap. 23, n. 2.

CHAPTER 32

1. "Listen, O heavens, and I will
speak;
and hear, O earth, the words of
my mouth.
2. Let my teaching *be as delightful*[1] as rain,
let my word *be accepted*[2] as dew;
as *the winds of the early showers that blow*[3] upon the
vegetation,
and as the droplets of the late rain[4] upon the grass.
3. For I *pray*[5] in the name of the
Lord;
offer greatness *before*[6] our Lord.
4. The *Mighty One,*[7] whose *deeds*[8] are perfect,
for all His ways are just,
a trustworthy God *from whom emerges*[9]

Notes, Chapter 32

[1]The Hebrew has: "descend," which may be appropriate for "rain" but too figurative for "teaching," hence the Targum paraphrases "be as delightful" which is equally relevant to the subject. The Frg. Tg. (P and V) as well as Tg. Neof. employ the same term (*ybsm*).

[2]The Hebrew has: "distil" which is applicable to "dew," whereas the Targum employs "accepted" which is equally applicable to "word." Tg. Ps.-Jon. and the Frg. Tg. (P, V) are similar but elaborate slightly—"be favorably accepted," while Tg. Neof. is identical to Tg. Onq.

[3]The Hebrew has: "showers" which the Targum here expands to refer to the winds of the early showers. The presence of "wind" in this paraphrase reflects a similar Rabbinic interpretation of this passage as expounded in the following Talmud—*b. B. Bath.* 25a "'As the showers (*śĕʿîrîm*) upon the vegetation' (Deut. 32:2), this is the east wind which rages through the world like a demon (*śaʿîr*)." As a syntactic consequence, the Targum then adds "that blows" to apply to the wind. Likewise Sifre (*Haʾăzînû* CCCVI, p. 340): "'As the showers upon the vegetation' (Deut. 32:2)—this is the east wind that darkens the sky like the showers."

[4]The Hebrew has *rĕḇîḇîm* "copious showers" which the Targum renders *rĕsîsê malqôš*—"droplets of rain," a translation also employed by the Pal Tgs.—Neof., Ps.-Jon. and the Frg. Tg. (P, V), each of which expand the paraphrase (with only slight variation among them). Tg. Neof. is representative—"as droplets of the late rain which come down and refresh the plants of the earth during the month of Nisan." The Syr. has *rsysy* only which, by itself, could mean "small drops," or "fine rain," or "gentle showers" (cf. Payne-Smith, *A Compendious Syriac Dictionary*. Oxford, 1957, p. 544, s.v. *rsysy'*). Cf. also Mic. 5:6, where it is similarly rendered by the Tg. Neb.

[5]See Exod. Chap. 8, n. 4.

[6]See Gen. Chap. 4, n. 1.

[7]The Hebrew *ṣûr*—"rock" is here, and throughout this chapter, interpretively rendered "the Mighty One" in referring to God. Even in vs. 37, where, according to most Rabbinic texts, it, and the preceding term—*'lhymw,* refers to God rather than to idols, for which cf. b. Git. 56b, Abot de R. Nat. Version B VII, p. 20, and Deb. Rab; ed. Lieberman, p. 22 where these words are attributed to Titus against God; Lam. Rab. Proem XXV, Exod. Rab. XV:16, Shoḥ. Tob LXV:1, p. 312, and Tanḥ (B) Ṣaw XVI, p. 21, where they are attributed to the nations of the world, called idolaters, against God. In Sifre Deut. CCCXXVIII *Haʾăzînû,* p. 378, the matter is the subject of a dispute—"'And it is said: Where are *ʾĕlôhēmô?*' (Deut. 32:37): R. Judah applied this to Israel, while R. Nehemiah applied it to the nations of the world. R. Judah says: In the future, Israel will say to the nations of the world: 'where are your consuls and generals?'"

[8]See Gen. Chap. 21, n. 7.

no wrong for He is righteous and truthful.

5. *They have corrupted themselves,*[10]
   the children no longer belong to Him[11]
   because they worshiped idols,[12]
   a generation *that changed its ways, and in turn were themselves transformed.*[13]
6. Here, is this the way that you repay the Lord,
   you people *who have accepted the Law*[14] but have not become wise?
   Is He not your father *and you belong to Him?*[15]
   Has He not made you and fashioned you?
7. Remember the days of old;
   consider the years of past ages;
   ask your father and he will inform you

Apparatus, Chapter 32

[a] A has: "the."

Notes, Chapter 32 (Cont.)

[9]An insertion, also present in Tg. Ps.-Jon. Tg. Neof. adds "falsehood" in a double reading. All of these insertions are implied in the concise poetic Hebrew text.

[10]The Hebrew has the singular: "it (has corrupted itself)" which could conceivably refer collectively to Israel; others (cited by S.R. Driver, *ICC-Deuteronomy, op. cit.*, p. 351) take "it" to refer to the "generation" mentioned at the end of the verse. The Targum, however, as do all the Pal. Tgs. as well as the Syr., the Sam. Tg., the LXX, and the Vg., renders into the plural referring to the "children" mentioned immediately thereafter.

[11]The Targum renders the Hebrew *lô* twice. As pointed out in the preceding note, it is rendered into the plural *lĕhôn* "themselves," thus drawing it to the preceding *šiḥēt*—"corrupted," as well as to what follows—"the children, no longer *belong to Him.*"

[12]The Hebrew has simply *mûmām* lit. "their defect," which is concise and consequently expanded defining the nature of their defect to be idolatry, as reflected in the Midrash—Exod. Rab. XLII:1 ". . . When God saw this, He said to Moses: 'Go down, for your people . . . have dealt corruptly (*šiḥēt*). The word *šiḥēt* signifies that they acted corruptly, as in the text "Its corruption is His' (Deut. 32:5). Not only they make an idol . . . ."

[13]The Hebrew has: "a crooked and twisted generation," a hendiadys that may be rendered "a greatly twisted generation." The Targum, however, treats each of the adjectives individually—*'iqqēš* "crooked" is interpreted to mean a generation that changed its ways (for the worse), whereas *up̠taltōl* "twisted," a mere synonym for "crooked," is here applied to the children of that generation, who underwent a change as a result of having changed their ways. The Pal. Tgs. (Frg. Tg. [P, V], Neof. and Ps.-Jon.), however, render the second half of this paraphrase differently, referring it not to the children who were changed, but to the order of the world's judgments—as can be seen from Tg. Neof. ". . . that crooked and twisted generation that has changed its ways; and, therefore, the orders of the world's judgements (the Frg. Tg. has simply 'orders of the world') have been changed towards it." Similarly vs. 20 below where Hebrew "perverse generation" is rendered "a *changed* generation."

[14]The Hebrew has: "foolish," which the Targum here renders "who have accepted the Law," opposite in meaning to what the text says, whereas everywhere else this word (*nāḇāl*) occurs it is rendered *ṭipšā'* ("foolish") in the Targum, as in vs. 21 below, by the Tgs. to Ps. 74:18 and Prov. 17:21; 30:22. Y. Koraḥ (*Marpe Lashon, op. cit.*, on this verse) has correctly explained this deviation in the Targum by pointing out that rendering *ṭipšā'* here would have destroyed the sense of the entire passage from the beginning of this verse—"Is this the way you repay the Lord you *foolish* people . . . " But that is precisely the nature of fools who do not recognize in gratitude God's favors. By translating *nāḇāl* "who accepted the Law," the Targum gives additional force to the beginning of the verse—even though you accepted the Law as a result of which you should surely have recognized God's favor, still, "you have not become wise." The Frg. Tg. (V) and Tg. Ps.-Jon. have both translations for *nāḇāl* here—"you foolish people, who have accepted the Law," while Tg.

your elders and they will tell you.
8. When the Most High gave nations
an inherited possession,
when He divided mankind,
He established the boundaries of the nations
according to the number
of Israelites.
9. For the Lord's portion is His people,
Jacob His *allotted*[16] inheritance.
10. *He supplied their needs*[17] in the territory of the wilderness,
a parched area, a region without water;[18]
He settled them all around His Shekhinah;[19]
He taught them the words of His[a] *Law;*[20]

Notes, Chapter 32 (Cont.)

Neof. and the Syr. have only "a foolish people." The Sifre (*ibid* CCCIX, p. 349) also makes the connection here between *nāḇāl* and the Law—"'a *nāḇāl* and unwise people' (Deut. 32:6) . . . now what caused Israel to be disgraceful (*mnwblym*) and foolish (*mtwpšym*), because they did not become wise through the words of the Law."

[15]The Hebrew *qnk* < *qnh* could mean "acquire," "possess," "buy," "create," although the last of the meanings is the most likely here in parallelism to the following "He has made you." Nevertheless, the Targum paraphrases in order to avoid attributing any human characteristics such as "possessing," "acquiring," or "buying" to God (although "creating" is entirely relevant to God, and Tg. Ps.-Jon., the Syr., and the Frg. Tg. [P] indeed use *qny* here). It is interesting to note the translations of Tg. Neof. and the Frg. Tg. (V) who render *qny* here with the meaning "possess" or "acquire" rather than "create," reserving the latter meaning for the following verb—"He made you," which they render by the Aramaic *bry,* and then use *škll* perfect for the last Hebrew verb in the verse. The Sifre (*ibid.,* p. 350) here interprets Hebrew *qnh* as "acquisition."

[16]The Hebrew *ḥéḇel* is here rendered *'db,* "lot," an interpretive translation which is paralleled in Sifre (*ibid.* CCCXII, p. 354) "Jacob is the *ḥéḇel* of his inheritance"—*ḥéḇel* means exlusively "lot." The Midrash then cites Jer. 10:16; Ps. 16:5; Jos. 17:5 to prove its point.

[17]The Hebrew has: "He found him" which the Targum here, as in Num. 11:22, renders "supplied their needs," i.e., maintained them, a translation shared here only by the LXX which has αὐτάρκησεν αὐτόν—"He maintained them." This deviant translation for Hebrew *mṣ'*—"find" in conjunction with the wilderness, is also present for Hebrew *yd'* where that verb is associated with the Israelites' trek in the wilderness in Deut. 2:7 above. The singular Hebrew pronoun "him" is here transformed into the plural to refer to the people, as well as throughout this chapter.

[18]The Hebrew has: "in an empty and howling waste" which the Targum renders to be a parched area without water, translating identically to the way he renders Deut. 8:15 where the phrase actually occurs in the Hebrew as a description for the wilderness. The three Hebrew terms here *tōhû, yělēl,* and *yěšîmōn* being descriptive terms of the wilderness, the first and third refer to its barren state, which the Hebrew *ṣimmā'ôn* in the above Deuteronomy passage parallels, thus providing a link between the two passages and the Targum's identical translation of both.

[19]The Hebrew has: "He surrounded them" which, in deference to God, is here paraphrased to transform God's surrounding them into their surrounding God's *Shekhinah.* So also Tg. Neof. "He settled them all around His *Yěqar Shekhinah."* The Frg. Tg. is similar but not identical, P—"He surrounded them with His *Yěqār Shekhinah"* and V—"He circumvented them with the clouds of His *Yěqār Shekhinah."* The Sifre (*ibid.* CCCXIII, p. 356) also avoids the idea of God Himself doing the surrounding by interpreting "He surrounded them with standards, three from the north, three from the south, three from the east, three from the west."

[20]The Hebrew *ybwnnhw* < *byn* "discern," "be intelligent," "instruct," is here translated by the Targum to be associated with the instruction of the Law.

He guarded them like the pupil of their eye.

11. Like an eagle that rouses its nestling,
hovering over its young,
it spreads its wings *receiving*[21] them,
then carrying them on the strength of its *pinions.*[22]

12. The Lord is going to *settle them in isolation in the world which is destined to be renewed,*[23]
whereas *idol worship will not remain in existence*[24] *before*[6]
Him.

13. *He settled them over the powerful ones of*[25]
the earth
and fed them the plunder of the enemies;[26]
He gave them the plunder of the rulers

Notes, Chapter 32 (Cont.)

[21]See Gen. Chap. 4, n. 8.

[22]See Gen. Chap. 21, n. 7.

[23]The Hebrew has: "The Lord alone led him." The Targum transforms this verb into the future and expands the phrase to refer to settlement in the World to Come. This Aggadic interpretation is reflected in the Sifre (*ibid.* CCCXV, p. 357) "'The Lord alone led them' (Deut. 32:12). Said the Holy One blessed be He to them: Just as you lived isolated in this world and did not benefit at all from the (other) nations, *so I am going to settle you in isolation in the future* (world), and not one of the (other) nations will benefit from you at all."

[24]See Introduction VII A.3.

[25]The Hebrew has: "He made him ride on the high places." As Löwenstein (*Nefesh Ha-Ger, op. cit.*, p. 68f) correctly pointed out that the reference is here to the Amorite kings—Siḥon and Og—the most powerful kings of their times whose defeat and subsequent submission is described in Num. 21:21-35. Löwenstein (note, p. 68) points to Ps. 136:18 "and He killed powerful kings" followed by (vs. 19) "Siḥon the Amorite king" and vs. 20 "Og king of Basham." He emphasizes that vs. 10 above dealing with God's maintenance of Israel in the wilderness corresponds to vs. 16 in Ps. 136, and from there on there are various typical parallels between the two Biblical passages.

[26]The Hebrew has: "and fed him the fruits of the fields." According to Löwenstein (*op. cit.*, p. 69) this corresponds to Pss. 135:12; 136:21, 22 "and He gave their land as an inheritance; as an inheritance to His servant Israel" referring to the land of the aforementioned kings which was given to the two and a half tribes in Transjordan (cf. Num. 32:33). The connection between the Hebrew and the Targum is further underscored by Löwenstein, who cites Deut. 2:35a (and 3:7 for that matter as well) where the plunder of Siḥon and Og's cattle is described in connection with ***śādāy*** in the present verse; ***śādāy*** referring to the cattle of the field as in Ps. 8:8b where the identical word occurs in the phrase ***bahămôt śādāy*** which is in synonymous parallelism with sheep and cattle in 8a.

[27]The Hebrew has: "He fed him honey from the rock and oil from the flinty rock." Löwenstein (*op. cit.*, p. 70f) here connects these two statements with Deut. 2:35b "and the plunder of the cities which we captured," the first of the two referring to the open cities which were not so hard to conquer as a rock—*séla'*, which is less hard than a *ḥalāmîš*—"a flinty rock"; the second "the properties . . . of strong towns" which are here compared to the flinty rock; these were harder to conquer, yet God helped them capture all of them (Deut. 3:4, 5).

[28]The Hebrew "curd of oxen and milk of flocks; with the fat of lambs and rams, as well as bulls of Bashan and he-goats; with the fat of kernels of wheat" is here further paraphrased according to Löwenstein (*op. cit.*, p. 71f) referring back to Deut. 3:7b "and the plunder of the cities which we captured," which according to him is a general statement that Moses in the present song, enumerates in detail. In 13b above he enumerates the plunder of the inhabitants of the cities, whereas in the present verse the plunder involves the stored

of cities
and the properties of the inhabitants of strong towns. [27]

14. *He gave them the plunder of their kings*
and rulers,
together with the wealth of their nobles and their mighty ones,
the people of their territories, their possessions,
together with the plunder of their soldiers and camps; [28]
and the blood of their warriors was spilled like
water. [29]

15. *Then Israel became wealthy*[30] and kicked;
it became prosperous as well as powerful,
and acquired property; [31]
then he abandoned *the worship of*[32] God who created him,

Notes, Chapter 32 (Cont.)

wealth of the Amorite kings—Siḥon and Og, the connecting point being the word *bāqār*—"oxen," which the Midrash (Num. Rab. XIII:14) associates with kingship, citing the present verse and Targum thereof—"'*Baqar*'(Num. 7:17) cannot but signify kingship, as is borne out by the text, 'the curd of oxen and the milk of flocks' (Deut. 32:14) which is rendered in Aramaic: 'He gave them the plunder of their kings.'" The phrase "fat of lambs and rams" is translated as a reference to "the wealth of their nobles and their mighty ones" with the following Hebrew *bĕnê bāšān* identifying these aforementioned as being the people of their territories, i.e., Bashan, as Deut. 3:1-3 refers to Og and Bashan. The Hebrew "he-goats" is rendered "their possessions" as in Isa. 10:9 where the Hebrew *'attûdê* "is translated—"those rich in possessions" by the Tg. Neb. Hebrew "fat" is again rendered "plunder," and *kilyôt ḥiṭṭāh*—"kernels of wheat" is translated as depicting "their soldiers and their camps."

The Sifre (*ibid.* CCCXVII, p. 360) interprets many of the terms in this verse to refer to various commanders and government officials, some of which parallel the translation of the Targum discussed above.

"'the curd of oxen'—these are their appointed government officials (the Midrash uses the Greek ὑπατικος "and their generals.")

'with the fat of the kidneys'—these are their commanders over a thousand soldiers (χιλιάρχοι)

'and rams'—these are their commanders over a hundred soldiers (the *centurions*)

... 'and he-goats'—these are their senators (σύγκλητος)."

[29]The Hebrew "and from the blood of grapes you drank wine" is here paraphrased—the grapes depicting the warriors of these nations, whose blood will be spilled as abundantly as water. Berkowitz (*Ote Or* in *Leḥem We-Simla.* Wilna, 1850-55, p. 25) has plausibly suggested that the Hebrew *ḥāmer* here refers to the earth (as in Gen. 14:10) with the verb *tišteh* having the earth as its subject, the message being that the earth would drink the wine, the wine here symbolizing the blood of the warriors which will be spilled onto the earth as abundantly as water—the figure of speech as in Deut. 15:23 "you shall spill on the ground like water."

[30]The Hebrew has: "So Jeshurun grew fat and kicked." The name Jeshurun is here rendered "Israel" as well as in 33:5, and 26 below, as well as by several mss. (listed by Sperber in his apparatus of *The Bible in Aramaic*, Vol. III—The Latter Prophets. Leiden [E.J. Brill], 1962, p. 89) in Isa. 44:2 where this name is parallel to Jacob, which in turn is parallel to Israel in Isa. 44:1. The verb "grew fat" is rendered by the Targum "became wealthy," an interpretation similar to the one given to the passage in the following Sifre (*ibid.* CCCXVIII, p. 361) "'So Jeshurun grew fat and kicked' Satiation is proportional to rebelliousness." Likewise, Sifre (*Éqeb* XLIII, p. 92) "'when you have eaten your fill ... beware lest your heart grow haughty ...' (Deut. 8:12, 13). He said to them: Beware lest you rebel against God, since rebelliousness against God only grows out of satiation."

[31]The Hebrew "you grew fat, and gross, and coarse" is here paraphrased in line with the preceding to symbolize the state of becoming prosperous, powerful, and wealthy in property.

[32]See Introduction VII B.3.

and caused provocation before[33] *the Mighty One*[7] *who redeemed Him.*[34]

16. They caused jealousy *before Him*[6]
in worshiping idols,[35]
with abominations they caused provocation
before Him.[6]

17. They sacrificed to demons *for whom there is no need,*[36]

[b] So also T, j, and i, whereas Sperber's main text has: "their."

[c] c has: "created."

[d] D has the plural.

[e] D adds: "the worship of."

Notes, Chapter 32 (Cont.)

[33]The Hebrew verb *wayĕnabbēl* having God as its direct object is somewhat toned down in translation—"caused provocation before," in order to avoid the association of the root of the verb *nbl* "disgrace" with God. Furthermore, Rabbi Dustai relates this Hebrew verse to Jer. 14:21 where *n'ṣ* "spurn" stands in direct synonymous parallelism with it (Sifre *Ha'azînû,* p. 363). For *n'ṣ* see Num. Chap. 14, n. 8.

[34]The Hebrew "his salvation" is rendered into a *nomen agentis* and treated as if the Hebrew root were *g'l* "redeem" instead of *yš'*. The close association of *ṣûr* with *g'l* is explicitly brought out in Ps. 19:15 where the Hebrew *ṣûrî wĕgô'ălî* referring to God is rendered *tûqpî upārîqî*—"my strength and my Redeemer" by the Tg. Ket. there.

[35]The Hebrew *bĕzārîm* ("with alien things") is here associated with the technical term for idolatry in Rabbinic literature—*'abôdāh zārāh* ("alien worship"), for which see Introduction VII A.3. The Sifre (*ibid.*) similarly relates this term to idolatry.

[36]The Hebrew has: "no gods" which the Targum renders interpretively to mean "for whom there is no need" in agreement with the following Sifre (*ibid.,* p. 364): "'They sacrificed to demons (which are) no gods' (Deut. 32:17). If they had worshiped the sun, the moon, the stars, and the planets, or *things for which there was a need* in the world and through whom there was a benefit in the world, the jealousy would not have been twofold; rather they worship things which, not only do not benefit them, but cause them harm."

[37]The Hebrew has: "who *came* only recently," which due to the attribution of the verb "come" to idols, was accordingly paraphrased "who *were made* only recently" by the Targum and Tg. Ps.—Jon., and "who *were created*" by Tg. Neof. and the Frg. Tg. (V).

[38]The Hebrew has: *śĕ'ārûm,* on which the Ancient Versions offer a variety of meanings—the Syr. "fear" (*dḥl*), the LXX "know" (ἤδεισαν) and the Vg. "worship" (*coluerunt*). The Targum, as do all the Pal. Tgs. (Neof., Ps.-Jon., and the Frg. Tg. [V]), renders "bother with," which is similar to the Sifre interpretation here (*ibid.*) "to perceive if there is any need for them or not." Driver (*Deuteronomy: ICC, op. cit.,* p. 363) associates this meaning, which is essentially the one used in the LXX, with Arabic *šáhara*—"to perceive" and Aramaic *s'r*—"to inspect."

[39]The Hebrew has: "forgotten" which Tgs. Ps.-Jon., Neof., and the Syr. all render literally, whereas Tg. Onq. and the Frg. Tg. (V) render "abandoned," perhaps as Löwenstein (*Nefesh Ha-Ger, op. cit.,* p. 76) points out, to avoid duplication of the same verb used in the first half of this verse.

[40]The Hebrew has: "gave birth (to you)" which, due to its anthropomorphic implications is here rendered interpretively "made" (or "created" according to one version, for which see Apparatus, note *c*). The other Aramaic versions also deviate here, the Syr. having "made you glorious," the Pal. Tgs. (Ps.-Jon., Neof., the Frg. Tg. [V, P]) "who made you with many cavities (< *ḥll*)."

[41]See Gen. Chap. 29, n. 8.

[42]Although everywhere else that Hebrew *n'ṣ* occurs it is rendered by the expression "caused provocation before," here the Targum does not use it because it is used immediately thereafter and thus avoids duplication of it.

along with the fury of the *serpents*[51]
that glide in the dust.
25. Outside the sword consumes;
inside there is fear of *death*[52]—
their *young men*[22] as well as their *young women,*[22]
their *sucklings*[22] along with
their *aged.'*[22]
26. I said, '*My anger will affect them,*[53]
and I will destroy them;[54]
I will abolish their memory from mankind.
27. Were it not that the fury of the enemy were *accumulated,*[55]
lest *the adversary claims superiority,*[56]
lest they say: Our hand has prevailed *for us,*[57]
none of this is from before the Lord.[58]

Notes, Chapter 32 (Cont.)

The Pal. Tgs. (Ps.-Jon., Neof. and the Frg. Tg. [V]) are similar in their translation, with Ps.-Jon. being more elaborate with Aggadic additions than the others.

[51]The Hebrew "those who glide" is specified in the Targum as well as in Tgs. Neof. and the Frg. Tg. (V) to refer to "serpents," in Tg. Ps.-Jon. to "venomous spirits." Cf. Ber. Rab. III:15, p. 56 (to Gen. 3:15) where the serpent is also explicitly stated as being the one that glides in the dust, in citing the present verse.

[52]The Hebrew has simply *'êmāh* "terror," "fear" which the Targum expands to "fear of death," as do the Frg. Tg. (V), and Tgs. Neof. and Ps.-Jon., the latter even using the identical Aramaic term for "fear of" (*ḥrgt*) as does Tg. Onq. The association of *'êmāh* with death does occur once, in Ps. 55:5, "and the fear of death has fallen over me." Cf. also Jer. 9:20, where the verse "death has come up to our windows" is cited in conjunction with the present verse in the Talmud (b. B. Qam. 60b).

[53]The Hebrew *'ap̱'êhem* is connected by the Targum to the noun *'ap̱* "anger" and rendered similarly to the Sifre (*ibid.* CCCXXII, p. 370) "'I said *'ap̱'êhem* (Deut. 32:26)—I intended with My anger to make them non-existent." Cf. also Ber. Rab. on Gen. 45:8, p. 212. The Frg. Tg. (V) likewise renders "I said by My *Memra* to bring anger upon them."

[54]This phrase occurs in Tg. Neof. as a translation for *'ap̱'êhem* and appears to be redundant here, unless it constitutes (an unattested) variant translation for *'ap̱'êhem* in Onqelos as well, thus resulting in a conflation of two variants—the first being "My anger will affect them" which has its parallel in the Frg. Tg. (V) cited in the preceding note.

[55]For the Hebrew *'āgûr* the Targum employs *kĕnîš* "accumulate," which finds a parallel in the following Sifre (*ibid.* CCCXXII, p. 371) "the expression *'āgûr* means exclusively 'to accumulate (*knws*)." The Sifre then proceeds to cite Prov. 30:1 and Ps. 55:16 as proof.

[56]The Hebrew has: "their enemies should behave strangely." Rashi explains the Hebrew *yĕnakkĕrû* to mean— "lest they treat the matter as arising from a stranger by attributing their power to a stranger, to whom the greatness, however, does not actually belong." One may take Rashi a step further in identifying that stranger as themselves, thus resulting in "a claim of superiority" on their own part as the verse actually continues "(it is) our hand that has prevailed for us." This may very well have been the intention of the Targum in his translation here.

[57]An insertion implied in the Hebrew.

[58]The Targum paraphrases the Hebrew: "and the Lord did not do any of this" by the introduction of the particle *qdm*—"before" (for which see Gen. Chap. 4, n. 1), thus avoiding the association of action with God but rather that all was caused by God, as in Gen. 45:8 "but God (did)," where the Targum likewise renders "but it was from *before* the Lord."

28. For they are a people who waste advice,
    having no sense.
29. Had they been wise and considered this,
    had they deliberated as to what their destiny will be;
30. How could one pursue a thousand
    and two put ten thousand to flight;
    lest their *Mighty One*[7] had *surrendered*[59]
    them and the Lord had delivered them up.
31. For their strength is not like our strength
    and our enemies are *our*[60]
    judges.

Apparatus, Chapter 32 (Cont.)

[h] c has the singular.

[i] Rashi has: "chastisement" reading *kmrdwthwn* instead of *kmrrthwn.*

[j] A has the plural.

Notes, Chapter 32 (Cont.)

[59]The Hebrew "sold them" was felt by the Targum to be too coarse as applying to God and thus rendered by the more general "surrendered" (*msr*) implied by the figurative Hebrew term here. Tg. Ps.-Jon. likewise employs the Aramaic root (*msr*), whereas the Syr. uses the *aphel* of *šlm* with the same meaning, the same root used by the Targum at the end of this chapter for Hebrew ***hisgîrām*** **"delivered them up"; the Pal. Tgs.** (Frg. Tg. [V] and Neof.) employ *msr* for the end of the verse and *šbq* "abandon" in the present case.

[60]The Hebrew does not have the first plural pronominal suffix but implies it. The Targum, as well as the Tgs. Ps.-Jon., Neof., and the Frg. Tg. (P, V) all supply it.

[61]The Hebrew has: "For their vine is from Sodom, from the vineyards of Gomorrah; for their grapes are grapes of gall, their clusters are bitter." The Targum interprets this verse in terms of the punishment that will be meted out to Israel, comparing it to the severity of the punishment that was given to Sodom and Gomorrah. The Pal. Tgs. (Frg. Tg. [V], Neof., and Ps.-Jon.) differ in that they interpret it in terms of a comparison between the deeds and thoughts of Israel and those of Sodom and Gomorrah; only in the last part of the work do the Pal. Tgs. parallel Tg. Onq. in dealing with the retribution motif. Tg. Neof. is representative of the Pal. Tgs. and hereby follows: "For the works of this people are comparable to the works of the people of Sodom, and their thoughts are comparable to the thoughts of the people of Gomorrah. Their works are evil works, and in accordance with their evil works shall retribution be exacted of them." The Frg. Tg. (V) stays close to the Hebrew in the last part of the verse—"their deeds are evil deeds, which bereave and embitter them," thus interpeting the word *'aškĕlôt* "clusters" from the root *škl* "to be bereaved" and *mĕrōrōt* literally. Tg. Ps.-Jon. parallels Tg. Onq. partially following the Gomorrah comparison in that the Hebrew "their grapes are grapes of gall" is rendered by Onq. "their plagues are as harmful as the heads of serpents," and by Ps.-Jon. "their thoughts are as harmful as the heads of poisonous serpents." The interpetation of this verse in terms of retribution may perhaps be related to the association of the retribution motif with a cup of wine, occurring in various instances throughout the Biblical text. Prominent among these are Ps. 75:19—"For in the hand of the Lord there is a cup, and the wine is red; it is full of mixture; and He pours out of the same; but the dregs thereof, all the wicked of the earth shall wring <them> out, and drink them"; and Jer. 25:15—"For thus says the Lord God of Israel to me: Take the wine-cup of this fury at My hand, and cause all the nations to whom I send you to drink it." Cf. also Isa. 51:17, 22; and Lam. 4:21. The cup motif does indeed occur in the following verse in translation for Hebrew "wine."

[62]The Hebrew has: "their wine," which is here interpretively rendered "cup of punishment," an association also prominent in Ps. 48:8, Jer. 25:15 and in the Song of the Vineyard (Isa. 27:3). Cf. also Isa. 28:13 and preceding note. Tg. Ps.-Jon. here calls it "the cup of malediction that the wicked will have to drink on the day of their punishment."

32. *For their punishment will be like the punishment of the people of*[61]
Sodom,
and their chastisement like that of the people of[61] Gomorrah;
their plagues are as harmful as the heads of serpents, and the retribution for their deeds[61]
<as deadly> as their *venom.*[i]
33. *The cup of their punishment is like*[62] the venom of serpents,
and *like*[63] the *head*[j] of the cruel adder reptiles.
34. Indeed *all their deeds*[64] are *revealed*[65] *before Me,*[6]
sealed up in My storehouses *for the day of judgment.*[66]
35. *Before Me*[6] is *punishment*[67]
and I will dispense <it> at the time *when they will be banished from their land;*[68]
for the day of their ruin is close,
as is the swiftness <for it to happen> that is in store for them.
36. For the Lord will judge *the case of*[69] His people
and *the cause of*[70] His *righteous*[71] servants will be *avenged,*[71]

Notes, Chapter 32 (Cont.)

[63]An insertion, converting the Hebrew metaphor into a simile.

[64]The vague Hebrew "it" is here specified to refer to "all their deeds," where in the Frg. Tg. (V, P) and Tg. Neof. "it" is interpreted to refer to "the cup of punishment for the wicked."

[65]The figurative "sealed up" is here rendered "revealed" instead of literally, in order to avoid duplication with the following phrase where the literal *gĕnîzîn* is used.

[66]An addition, also present in Tg. Neof. and the Frg. Tg. (P, V) in the form of "the day of the great judgment." The following Sifre (*ibid.* CCCVII, p. 345) reflects it as well: ". . . now how do we know that the wicked have not taken any of their (reward) in this world, as it says: 'Lo, it is concealed with Me, sealed up in My storehouses' (Deut. 32:34). When will both (the righteous and the wicked) take (their reward)? 'For all His ways are just' (Deut. 32:4) *in the future when He will sit on the throne* of judgment sitting in deliberation over every single one, then He will give to him what is due to him."

[67]See Gen. Chap. 4, n. 10.

[68]The figurative Hebrew "when their foot falters" is here rendered into its intended meaning which, according to the Targum, refers to the time that "they will be banished from their land."

[69]An insertion implied in the concise Hebrew text, also present in the Pal. Tgs., Ps.-Jon., Neof. and the Frg. Tg. (V), where "His people" are identified as Israel. Onq. makes no such identification, and the Sifre (*ibid.* CCCXXVI, p. 377), in fact, interprets it to refer to other nations rather than to Israel, which, according to Sifre, are mentioned in the next clause as "His servants." According to the Frg. Tg. (V), Tg. Neof., and Tg. Onq. likewise take the latter clause to refer to Israel since they add the qualifier "righteous" to "His servants."

[70]This insertion differs from that of Tg. Ps.-Jon.—"for the evil that He will decree upon" and that of Tg. Neof. "the humiliation of." The nature of the insertion here appears to depend on how the translator understood Hebrew *yiṯnĕḥām* further on in the verse. Tg. Onq. rendered it "avenge" so inserted *pûr'anûṯā'*—"cause," thus—the cause of His righteous servants will be avenged; "Tg. Neof. translated it "show compassion for," so inserted *'elbôn*—"humiliation of," thus—"He will show compassion for the humiliation of His righteous servants"; while Tg. Ps.-Jon. rendered it "there will be regret before Him" so inserts "for the evil that He will decree upon," thus—"and for the evil that He will decree upon His servants there will be regret before Him." The latter interpretation is found in the following Sifre (*ibid.*) ". . . and when the Holy One, blessed be He, judges Israel as though as it were possible, as it were, there is regret before Him, as it says: 'and for His servants *yiṯnĕḥām'* (Deut. 32:36) and *nḥmh* only means 'regret,' as it says: 'For I regretted that I made them' (Gen. 6:7), and as it says: 'I regret that I crowned Saul as king' (1 Sam. 15:11)."

[71]See n. 69 and 70 above.

for it is revealed before Him,[41] *that at the time that the assault of the enemy will overpower them,*
they will wander about and feel
abandoned.'[72]

37. Then he will say, 'Where is their Deity, the *Mighty One*[7]
in whom they trusted?'
38. 'The fat of whose sacrifices they ate,
the wine of whose libation they drank; let them now arise and help you,
and be a shield for you.
39. See now that I, I am He,
and there is no god *beside Me,*[73]
I put to death and I bring to life,
I do indeed wound, but <also> I heal,
and none can deliver from
My hand.
40. *For I have established the place of My Shekhinah in heaven,*[74]
and I declare: I exist forever.
41. *If My sword is doubly revealed,*
like the sight of lightning from one end of heaven to the other end

Notes, Chapter 32 (Cont.)

[72]The Hebrew has: "that their strength is gone, and neither guarded (= slave) or forsaken (free) is left." The Targum here attempts to explain the concise poetic phrase *kî 'ozlat yād*—"that their strength was gone" as being the result of the enemy's assault which overpowered them. The Tg. Ps.-Jon. is even more explicit here—"at the time that they will sin, the enemy's assault will overpower them and thus support from them (lit. their hands) will be taken away." The last part of the verse *wĕ'ěpes 'āṣûr wĕ'āzûb* is understood by the Targum to describe two states of being—the first one *wĕ'ěpes 'āṣûr* describes someone who is tied down, which the Targum renders "wander about," the second is rendered literally except pluralized as is the entire phrase. Berkowitz (*Ḥalifot Semalot.* Wilna, 1874, p. 144) points out that Hebrew *'ěpes* appears to negate only the first of the two passive participles according to the Targum. Yet, he cites 2 Kgs. 14:26 where *'ěpes* precedes both participles in this identical expression which would then appear to make the second one difficult to understand if *'zb* had the meaning "to abandon." He therefore concludes on the basis of Exod. 23:5 and Neh. 3:8 that this particular Hebrew root could also mean "to help," thus in the Kings passage cited above the negated *'zb* would make sense—"unaided." Similarly, Berkowitz reasons, the Aramaic *šbq* could denote both "abandon" and "help." J. Behaq (*Tosefot Ū-Milu'im.* Warsaw, 1898, p. 18) points to Ezek. 16:22 where the Tg. Neb., as in the case of 2 Kgs. 14:26 and Tg. Onq. in the present verse, uses this Aramaic expression "wandering about and abandoned" for the Hebrew *'êrōm wĕ'eryāh*—"naked and bare."

[73]The Hebrew *'immādî* is here rendered interpretively to mean "beside Me" rather than by its more common meaning "with me" (for which cf. Gen. 3:12; 19:19; 20:9). Tgs. Neof., Ps.-Jon., the Frg. Tg. (V), and the Syr. likewise have *bar minnî* here, as do the Vg. (*praeter me*) and LXX (πλὴν). Only the Sam. Tg. has "with me" (*'mmî*).

[74]The Hebrew "Lo, I raise My hand to heaven" due to the anthropomorphism involved ("hand"), and the peculiar situation of God raising His hand towards heaven, an act more applicable to man, is here paraphrased describing an act more suitable to God. The Pal. Tgs. (Neof., Ps.-Jon., and the Frg. Tg. [V]) all render this figurative expression as the standard oath formula.

[75]The Hebrew has: "When I sharpen My flashing sword," which involves human action on the part of God and is consequently paraphrased by the Targum into a passive scene involving the revealed sword of God. The Targum treated Hebrew *šannôṯî* (< *šnn*) as derived from *šnh* "repeat," "double," hence "doubly revealed," then augments this thought by further adding—"like the sight of lightning from one end of heaven to the other end of heaven," here expounding on the Hebrew *brq*.

(*of heaven*)[75]

and My hand *will prevail*[76] in judgment, I will repay vengeance to those who hate Me

and will recompense My enemies.

42. I will make drunk My arrows with blood,

and My sword *will carry out execution among the nations,*[77]

from the blood of those slain and the captives, *to the removal of the crowns*[78]

from the head of the *adversary and the enemy.*[79]

43. Give praise to His people, O you nations,

for the *cause*[80] of His *righteous*[71] servants

will be avenged; moreover the punishment will be reverted to His enemies,

and so He will atone *for His land and for His people.'"*[81]

44. Then Moses came, he and Joshua, son of Nun, to recite all the words of this song of praise *before*[6] the people. 45. When Moses finished reciting all these words to the Israelites, 46. he said to them, "Take to heart all the words that I warn you this day; that

Notes, Chapter 32 (Cont.)

76The anthropomorphism of the Hebrew "and My hand will grasp" is somewhat diminished, though not totally eliminated, by the translation "My hand will prevail" in the Targum as well as in Tg. Ps.-Jon. Similarly in Tg. Neof. and the Frg. Tg. (V), both of which make it the "right hand."

77The Hebrew: "will devour flesh" is a figure of speech paraphrased by the Targum to refer to God carrying out His "execution among the nations." The Pal. Tgs. are remarkably literal here. The Sifre (*ibid.* CCCXXXII, p. 381), however, asks "'and My sword will devour flesh'—is it really possible for a sword to devour flesh?" Then goes on to answer: "It essentially means 'I will feed others from what My sword accomplishes.'"

78The Hebrew "from the bared head of the enemy" is concise and as Löwenstein (*Nefesh Ha-Ger, op. cit.*, p. 89) points out, according to the Targum the verse is to be rearranged in word order reading *pĕrāʿôt mēr'ôš 'owyēb* with *pĕrāʿôt* meaning "locks of hair," here symbolizing an ornamentation on the head, the equivalent of which, in the case of kings and rulers (of the enemy) would be the "crown."

79The Hebrew has simply: "the enemy," which the Targum appears to be rendering by a double translation, unless he translates the preceding *pĕrāʿôt* as enemy, too, as does the Sifre (*ibid.*, p. 382) in the last of many explanations of this word—"Another explanation for *mr'š prʿt 'wyb* (Deut. 32:42)—What was their reason for imputing all retributions on the head of the Pharaoh? Because he was the first to enslave Israel." The first enemy is thus the Egyptian Pharaoh.

80The Hebrew has: "blood," which the Targum renders "cause," undoubtedly by way of association with vs. 36 above where the phrase "the cause of His righteous servants" also occurs, although there "cause" exists only as an insertion in the Targum. The Frg. Tg. (V) has: "humiliation" (*ʿelbôn*), the identical term used by Tg. Neof. in vs. 36 above, while Tg. Neof. has both the literal rendering—"blood" and the interpretive translation—"humiliation"; Tg. Ps.-Jon. has only "blood." The double reading in Neof. appears to be a conflation of the two variants existing independently in the Frg. Tg. (V) and in Tg. Ps.-Jon.

81The Hebrew has: *'admāṯô ʿammô*—"his land, his people" an asyndeton, which could well be a construct genitive clause in the sense of "the land of His people," the reading of the Sam Heb. (which has *'dmt ʿmw*), the Sam. Tg. (*'rʿt ʿmh*), the Vg. (*terrae populi sui*); or in the conjunctive sense "his land and his people," the reading adopted by the Targum, the Syr., the Frg. Tg. (V), the Tg. Ps.-Jon., and the Tg. Neof. ("*the* land, and *the* people").

you should command your children to diligently observe all the words of this Law. 47. For this should not be an empty matter to you, for it is your very existence; for through this matter you will prolong <your> days in the land for which you are about to cross the Jordan to possess." 48. Then the Lord said to Moses on that very day as follows, 49. "Ascend this Mount of Ibraea—Mount Nebo, which is in the land of Moab opposite Jericho, and view the land of Canaan that I am giving to the Israelites as an inherited possession. 50. Then you will die on the mountain that you will ascend and be gathered to your people, as Aaron your brother died on Mount Hor and was gathered to his people. 51. Because *you acted deceitfully against*[k] *My Memra*[82] among the Israelites at the Waters of Contention—*Rekem*[83] <in> the Wilderness of Zin, not having sanctified Me among the Israelites. 52. Even if you will view the land from the other side you will not enter it—the land that I am giving to the Israelites."

CHAPTER 33

1. Now this is the blessing that Moses, the *prophet*[1] of the Lord, blessed the Israelites before his death.
2. He said,
"The Lord *revealed Himself*[2] from Sinai,
the splendor of His glory appeared to us[3] from Seir;
He revealed Himself[4] *through His power*[5] *on*[a] Mount Paran,

Apparatus, Chapter 32 (Cont.)

[k] i and n have: "rebelled (against)."

Apparatus, Chapter 33

[a] l has: "from," as does the Hebrew.

[b] G, V, and c actually add it.

Notes, Chapter 32 (Cont.)

[82]See Introduction VII D.1.
[83]See Gen. Chap. 14, n.8.

Notes, Chapter 33

[1]The Hebrew has: "man" which the Targum renders "prophet," and this Targumic tradition is also present in Tg. Ps.-Jon., the Frg. Tg. (V), and Tg. Neof. as well as in the Tg. Ket. to Ps. 90:1. A parallel Rabbinic tradition occurs in PR IV *Wayyiqqaḥ Eliyāhū*, p. 13a "You find that Moses and Elijah were alike in every respect: Moses was a prophet; Elijah was a prophet . . . . " Finally, there is the Biblical tradition in 34:10 below—"Never again did there arise in Israel a prophet like Moses." Cf. also 1 Sam. 2:27.

[2]See Exod. Chap. 20, n. 10.

[3]The anthropomorphic "He shone upon them" of the Hebrew is circumvented by the Targum who transforms the verb "shone," referring to God, into its related noun "the splendor of His glory" with the passive verb form "appeared," then adding "to us," an addition also present in the Syr. Cf. also Sifre (*Wez'ōt Habĕrāḵāh* CCCXLII, p. 395f) where the verb "revealed" is used as here.

and *with Him were myriads of*
holy ones;[6]
from the midst of the fire He gave the Law, written by His right hand."[7]
3. Indeed He loved them—*the tribes;*[8] all His holy ones—*the House of Israel;*[9]
with power did He bring <them>[h]
out of Egypt,[10]
and they were led beneath Your cloud;[11]

Notes, Chapter 33 (Cont.)

[4]The active "He appeared" of the Hebrew is transformed into the standard passive "He revealed Himself" with the addition of "through His power." Cf. also Sifre (*ibid.*) where the Hebrew verb *glh* (reveal) is used in the passive in describing God's appearance from Mt. Paran in this verse. The Syr. also makes this transformation of the Hebrew verb.

[5]An insertion recalling the display of God's power during the theophany at Sinai which is also known by the name Paran, as well as by three other names (for which cf. b. Šabb. 89a-b). Thus the Targum reflects a description of God's power during the giving of the Law as seen from Exod. 19:16, 18-19; 20:18. Similarly, the Tg. Neb. to Hab. 3:3" and the Holy One from Mt. Paran" renders "and the Holy One from Mt. Paran through eternal power." Furthermore, the following Rabbinic discussion concerning the giving of the Law indicates a certain display of power by God, especially the coercion tactic—b. 'Abod. Zar. 2b: "'The Lord came from Sinai and rose from Seir unto them, He shined forth from Mt. Paran' (Deut. 33:2). And it is also written 'God comes from Teman' (Hab. 3:3). What did He seek in Seir and what did He seek at Mt. Paran? R. Joḥanan says: This teaches us that the Holy One, blessed be He, offered the Torah to every nation and to every tongue, but none accepted it, until He came to Israel who accepted it . . . in commenting on the verse 'and they stood at the nether part of the mountain' (Exod. 19:17) R. Dimi b. Ḥama said: This teaches us that the Holy One, blessed be He, suspended the mountain over Israel like a vault, and said unto them: 'If you accept the Torah, it will be well with you, but if not, there you will find your grave.'"

[6]The Hebrew *wĕʾāṯāh* is here understood as *ʾt* "with" as if the Hebrew *wĕʾittô* "and with Him" with the following *mēriḇĕḇôt qṓdeš* rendered literally—"myriads of holy ones." So also the Syr., as well as the Pal. Tgs.—Ps.-Jon., Neof. and the Frg. Tg. (P, V), only the latter specifying "holy angels" instead of "holy ones."

[7]The Hebrew has: "from His right hand <came forth> a fiery law for them." The Targum here merely paraphrases the somewhat concise Hebrew wording and also points out that the law refers to the Torah—an equation also made in the following Midrash-Shoḥ. Tob X:1, p. 92 "and law means Torah, as it says: 'from his right hand (came forth) a fiery law for them.'" The Targum also adds that the Law (Torah) was *written* by the right hand. In this vein the Midrash (Tanḥ(A) *Yiṯrô* XVI) remarks that the Torah was all fire, its parchment being made of fire, its *script* was in fire, as well as its stitches (connecting the various parchment folios) was of fire, pointing to the present verse as proof.

[8]The Hebrew has: "people" which, according to the Targum here means the tribes (of Israel), an interpretation shared by the Sifre (*ibid.* CCCXLIV, p. 400): "'Indeed He loved the nations' teaching that God loved Israel (in a way) that He did not love any other nation or kingdom." The Frg. Tg. (V), Neof., and Ps.-Jon. similarly have His people—the House of Israel (Ps.-Jon.), the Israelites (Frg. Tg. [V], and Neof.); and Frg. Tg. (P) simply "the Israelites." Cf. also Mid. Tan. to Deut. XXXIII:3, p. 212 for a similar identification. Cf. also vs. 19, n. 49 below.

[9]An addition, also reflected in Sifre (*ibid.*) ". . . these are the leaders of Israel" (later specified as Moses and David).

[10]The Targum renders "in Your hand" by "with power" in order to avoid the anthropomorphism, then connects it with the following clause "did He bring them out of Egypt" which is an addition in the Targum recalling Exod. 13:10 "for with a mighty hand did the Lord bring you out of Egypt."

[11]The Hebrew has the difficult *tukkû* which the Targum rendered to mean "were led" in conjunction with the translation of the following word "at Your feet," which due to its anthropomorphism was rendered "Your cloud" (cf. Exod. 13:21; Neh. 9:21), thus continuing the sense of the preceding clause which dealt with God's redemption of Israel from Egypt. This thought is further continued in the last clause of this verse for which see next note.

they traveled by Your Memra.[12]

4\. Moses *gave*[13] us the Law,
He delivered it[13] as an inheritance to the congregation of Jacob.

5\. There will be a king over
Israel,[14]
when the heads of the people will have assembled,
the tribes of Israel together.

6\. May Reuben live *an everlasting life and not die a second death,*[15]
and may his descendants receive their inherited possession according to their number.[16]

7\. Now this he said of Judah,
"Accept, O Lord, the prayer of[17] Judah

Apparatus, Chapter 33 (Cont.)

[c] G adds: "to wage."
[d] G has: "his," as does the Hebrew.
[e] M, i, s, b, d_2, and g have: "tested" which is closer to the Hebrew in sense.

Notes, Chapter 33 (Cont.)

[12]The Hebrew *yiśśā' middabbĕrōtêkā* is here understood in the same way as in Num. 9:23 and consequently rendered by the Targum the same it is there rendered.

[13]The Hebrew has: "commanded" which the Targum here renders by the non-literal "gave," perhaps to serve as an associate parallel to "delivered" which he inserts in the second half of this verse. The Pal. Tgs., however, render the Hebrew literally by *pqd,* and insert "gave" in the latter half of the verse.

[14]See above Chap. 32, n. 30.

[15]The Hebrew has: "May Reuben live and not die." The Targum interprets the word "live" to mean "live forever," and the phrase "not die" to mean "not die a second death," an interpretation shared and expanded by the Pal. Tgs. (Ps.-Jon., Neof., the Frg. Tg. [P, V]) as follows: "May Reuben live in this world and may he not die a second death by which the wicked die in the world to come." Accordingly, the verse deals with both worlds—6a with the present world; 6b with the world to come. The Pal. Tgs. states this explicitly, while Tg. Onq. implies it nevertheless in more concise terms, while the Sifre (*ibid.* CCCXLVII, p. 404) does so partially: "'May Reuben live and not die' (Deut. 33:6) but he is dead! Then what does 'and not die' come to teach? In the world to come." Similarly, in Rabbinic literature we find the widespread tradition that Reuben will live in both worlds:

b. Sanh. 92a "Raba said: Whence is resurrection derived from the Torah? From the verse (Deut. 33:6) 'May Reuben live and not die,' meaning 'let Reuben live' in this world, 'and not die' in the world to come."

The answer minus the question is also to be found in: **Tanḥ(B)** ***Wayyeṣē'*** **XIV, p. 153; Agg. Ber. XLIX:3, p. 98; and Ber. Rab. XXXV:23, p. 158.**

[16]The Hebrew has: "and let his men be numbered." The Targum elaborates on the concise Hebrew statement explaining "men" (*mĕṯāw*) as referring to "his descendants" and "number' to mean that they should receive their inherited possessions according to their number. A somewhat similar interpretation may be seen in the following Midrash—Num. Rab. XIII:18 "'and let his men be numbered' (Deut. 33:6) i.e., 'may his descendants be included in the number of the other tribes, for all purposes.'"

[17]See Gen. Chap. 16, n. 1, 5.

[18]This insertion refers back to Gen. 49:8 which deals with Judah's war escapades. The Tg. Ps.-Jon. parallels Onqelos here, while Tg. Neof. and the Frg. Tg. mention war only towards the end of this verse.

[19]An addition, also in Tgs. Ps.-Jon. and Neof. which continues the thought of the preceding insertion, in that Judah's prayer upon going out to war for God to bring him back to his people should be "safely."

[20]The Hebrew has: "strive for him." The Targum renders the verb "strive" by the more militant "wreak

when he goes out to[c] *war*[18] and bring him back to his people *safely;*[19]
through his own hands, *wreak vengeance for him against his adversaries;*[20]
be a support *to him*[21] against *the*[d]
enemies."

8. Concerning Levi he said,
"<With> Your Thummim and Your Urim,
You clothed *the man who was found to be pious before You,*[22]
whom You tested at *Nisetha*[23] *and who was <found to be> perfect;*[24]
You *chose*[e] him at The Waters of Contention *and he was found to be loyal.*[25]

9. *One who showed no mercy for his father or his mother*
when they were condemned in judgment,
one who did not favor his brother
or his sons,[26]

Notes, Chapter 33 (Cont.)

vengeance" then expands the clause by adding "against his adversaries," implied in the concise poetic Hebrew, in order to balance the synonymous parallel in the following colon. All the Pal. Tgs. (Ps.-Jon., Neof. and the Frg. Tg. [V]) render similarly.

[21]An addition implied in the Hebrew, and also added in the Pal. Tgs. and the Syr.

[22]The Hebrew has: "your pious man." The Targum paraphrases this somewhat vague designation which assigns possession to God. Whenever that situation occurs in the text, the Targum usually paraphrases with *qdm*, for which cf. Exod. 3:1; 4:20; 8:15; 9:28; 40:38, just to cite a few cases. The Sifre (*ibid.* CCCXLIX, p. 408) likewise felt compelled to comment as follows: "'to your pious man' (Deut. 33:8), to the one to whom favors were granted by your children." The Ps.-Jon. Tg. renders similarly, while Tg. Neof. and the Frg. Tg. (V) have: "to Aaron the pious man," and the Frg. Tg. (P) has: "to the pious Aaron."

[23]See Exod. Chap. 17, n. 4.

[24]An insertion that follows naturally the preceding "whom You tested at Nisetha" and is explicitly stated in the following Sifre (*ibid.*) "'Whom You tested at Massah' (Deut. 33:8). Many tests have You given him, but he was found to be perfect throughout all of the tests." The Ps.-Jon. Tg. is identical to Onq. here, while Tg. Neof. and the Frg. Tg. (V) interpret this verse to refer to Aaron, adding "and he remained steadfast in the trial."

[25]This addition, also present in Tgs. Ps.-Jon., Neof., and the Frg. Tg. (V) complements the preceding addition.

[26]The Hebrew has: "One who said of his father and his mother—'I consider them not,' nor did he regard his brother or acknowledge his own children." This enigmatic passage is here partially clarified by the Targum who adds to the first of the three sections the significant statement "when they were condemned in judgment." He also paraphrases the rather figurative "I did not see them" into its intended meaning "he showed no mercy for." He then combines the second section, concerning the brothers with the third section, concerning the sons, into a single unit changing both verbal clauses into a common one—"who did not favor his brothers or his sons." These additions and changes still leave the passage somewhat vague; whereas the Pal. Tgs. are more elaborate here, pinpointing the precise historical event involved. Yet even these versions are unamimous, therefore the most complete of the versions—the Frg. Tg. (V) is hereby cited: "For it is said about the members of the tribe of Levi: 'He did not favor his father or his mother in the case of Tamar; nor was he partial to his brothers in the incident of the (golden) calf; nor did he have mercy upon his sons in the incident of Zimri." Apparently, Tg. Onq. here refers all three sections to the Golden Calf incident when the Levites were bid to execute everyone who participated in the worship of that idol, be it their own kin, friend, or neighbor (cf. Exod. 32:27-29). This approach is also reflected in the following Midrashim: Tanḥ(A) *Behaʿălôṯēḵā* VIII; Tanḥ(B) *Bammidbar* XXXII, p. 24f. and *Behaʿălôṯēḵā* XIII, p. 50f; and Num. Rab. XV:12; in all of the aforementioned the phrase "they did not favor" occurs, corresponding to the identical phrase used in the Targum here. Rabbinic support for the Pal. Tgs.' interpretation may be found in Ber. Rab. XXXVIII:24, p. 181.

for they observed *the charge of Your Memra*[27]
and did not alter*[28] Your covenant.

10. *Worthy are they who*[29] teach Your judgments to Jacob
and Your Law to Israel;
they place aromatic spices *before You*[30]
and a whole-offering *for goodwill*[31] on Your altar.

11. Bless, O Lord, his *possessions*[32]
and willingly accept the *offering*[33] of his hands;
break the loins of his adversaries
and of his enemies that they rise
no more."[34]

12. Concerning Benjamin he said,
"The beloved one of the Lord

Apparatus, Chapter 33 (Cont.)

[f] D has: "all the days."
[g] G and O have: "springs and depths."
[h] D omits.

Notes, Chapter 33 (Cont.)

[27]The Hebrew has: "Your word" which the Targum translates as Memra, as he did in 32:2 above where the Hebrew *'imrāh* refers to Moses' word and is rendered *mēmrî*. The Targum then adds *maṭrat* "the charge of" in view of the preceding verb *šāmrû* (= Aramaic *nāṭrû*) forming the genitive phrase *maṭrat mêmrāk* used in Gen. 26:5; Lev. 18:30; 22:9 (with the first person suffix) and Deut. 11:1 (with the third person suffix).

[28]The Hebrew has: "and observed Your covenant," which the Targum here avoids rendering literally as does the Syr., instead translating it by the corresponding negative "they *did not alter* Your covenant." A check in the Biblical concordance reveals that the Hebrew root *nṣr* used here in conjunction with "covenant," is indeed a rarity; the only other time it occurs throughout the entire Biblical text is in Ps. 25:10 (where, in contrast to here, the phrase is rendered literally by the Tg.Ket.). The standard root used to express "observance" of the covenant is *šmr* (cf. Gen. 17:9, 10; Exod. 19:5; Deut. 29:8; 1 Kgs. 11:11; Ezek. 17:14; Dan. 9:4; Pss. 103:18; 132:12), and the notion of breaking the covenant is always rendered by *šny* as in the Targum, for which cf. Lev. 26:15, 44 and Deut. 31:16, 20. The Targum thus simply borrowed a familiar phrase from the notion of breaking the covenant and applied it in a negative sense to the observance of the covenant in a case where an unfamiliar Hebrew root was used to express observance.

[29]An insertion, also present in the Frg. Tg. (V), and Tgs. Neof. and Ps.-Jon., which may simply be a way to point out that the emphasis is on the word "they," in that only the Levite Priests were qualified to render judgments and teach the Law to Israel as pointed out. This point emerges from the following Sifre (*ibid.* CCCLI, p. 408) "'They shall teach Your judgments to Jacob' (Deut. 33:10) teaching that all decisions should only emerge from their mouths, as it says: 'and by their word shall every controversy and every plague be decided' (Deut. 21:5)." The Talmud adds the Issakharites as being also qualified in this respect—

b. Yoma 26a "Raba said: You will not find any Rabbinical scholar giving decisions who is not a descendant from the tribe of Levi or Issakhar. 'Of Levi' as it is written 'They shall teach Your judgments to Jacob.'"

[30]The Hebrew "in Your nostril" which is anthropomorphic is paraphrased with *qdm* "before."

[31]An insertion which may be associated with the following Sifre (*ibid.*, p. 409) "Another explanation . . . 'and whole-offerings on your altar' (Deut. 33:10). These are the limbs of the burnt offerings," in view of the burnt offering always being described as "pleasing before the Lord" (cf. Lev. 1:9, 13, 17). The Frg. Tg. (V) and Tg. Ps.-Jon. insert likewise. The same insertion is made in vs. 19 below.

[32]See Gen. Chap. 21, n. 7, for the plural here. Furthermore, the translation "possessions" is also reflected in Sifre (*ibid.* CCCLII, p. 409) in contrast to "strength."

shall dwell in safety by Him;
He will shield him *every day*[f]
and will rest the *Shekhinah*[35] *in his territory."*[36]

13. Concerning Joseph he said,
"His territory is blessed *from before*[37] the Lord;
it produces[38] *precious goods*[32] through the dew of heaven *from above*[39]
and through the fountains of *deep springs*[g] *which flow from the depths of the earth*[38]
from below.[h]

14. *Moreover, it produces*[38] *precious goods*[32] *and yields from the bounteous harvest of*[40] the sun;
it produces[38] *precious goods*[32] *at the beginning of each month,*[41]

15. and from the top of the early mountains,
and *precious goods*[32] from the everlasting hills,

16. and from the best of the earth and its fullness,
He, whose Shekhinah is in heaven, is content, and He revealed Himself to Moses in the bush;[42]

Notes, Chapter 33 (Cont.)

[33]The Hebrew "work," "undertaking" is here interpretively rendered to mean "offering" in conjunction with the predicate *tirṣeh* which the Targum translates into sacrifical terminology "willingly accept." Tg. Neof. and the Frg. Tg. (V) render similarly, while Tg. Ps.-Jon. elaborates—"the offering of the hands of Elijah the priest which he will offer on Mt. Carmel accept willingly. . . . "

[34]The Hebrew *min* is here understood as "from (rising)" i.e., not to rise, to rise no more.

[35]See Introduction VII D.3.

[36]The Hebrew "his shoulders" is figurative, and is here transformed to refer to Benjamin's territory; so also Tg. Ps.-Jon., and the Frg. Tg. (V) and Tg. Neof. (in the latter the *Yeqar Shekhina* is used).

[37]See Gen. Chap. 4, n. 1.

[38]An insertion to define the concise Hebrew text.

[39]An addition influenced by Gen. 49:25, where the phrase "of heaven from above" exists in the Hebrew.

[40]The Hebrew has: "with the bounteous yields of the yield of the sun." The Hebrew word "yield of"—*tĕḇû'ōt* appears to be rendered here by a double translation—*'alĕlān,* the standard term for it (for which cf. Gen. 47:2, 4; Lev. 25:16, 17; Deut. 14:22 for selected examples) and the term used here by the Syr. and the Pal. Tgs.—Neof. and the Frg. Tg. (V); the other translation is *yĕbûl,* used by Tg. Ps.-Jon. and even occuring in the Hebrew at times for *tĕḇû'āh* (for which cf. Lev. 26:4, 20; Deut. 11:17; 32:22, in each case the Targum renders by the noun *'llt'*).

[41]The Hebrew has: "yield/produce of the moons" which the Targum (as do Tgs. Neof., Ps.-Jon., and the Frg. Tg., all of which add "every") renders interpretively to mean every beginning of each month, by translating Hebrew *géreš* "yield/produce" to be basically understood as deriving from the root *grš* "to drive away," as one month "replaces" or "drives away" the next, hence, from beginning of a month to the next.

[42]The Hebrew has: "and the favor of Him who dwelt in the burning bush." The Tg. renders *šōḵnî* "who dwelt in" as referring to God's *Shekhinah* but hurriedly adds the qualifying clause "which really exists in heaven," and that it existed in the burning bush only for Moses' sake, where God revealed Himself to him.

may *all*[43] these come *upon the head of*
Joseph,
a man distinguished among[44] his
brothers.

17. *The greatest among his sons,*[45] who has splendor,
mighty deeds were done for him by the One who has power
and dignity;[46]
by his might he kills[45]
nations instantaneously, *till*[47] the ends of the
earth;

Apparatus, Chapter 33 (Cont.)

[i] j omits "Israel."

Notes, Chapter 33 (Cont.)

The last point is also emphasized in the following Sifre (*ibid.* CCCLIII, p. 414), "'and the favor of Him who dwelt in the burning bush' (Deut. 33:16)—which fulfilled the will of the One who was revealed to Moses at the burning bush." Tg. Ps.-Jon. equals Onqelos here adding only *Yeqar* to *Shekhinah,* an element also present in Tg. Neof. and the Frg. Tg. (V), both of which omit the name Moses here.

[43]An insertion which exists in a longer addition throughout all of the Pal. Tgs.—Neof., Ps.-Jon. and the Frg. Tg., of which Tg. Neof. is hereby cited: "May *all these* blessings come and may they become the crown of dignity on the head of Joseph."

[44]See Gen. Chap. 49, n. 67.

[45]The Hebrew has: "(Like a) firstborn bull," a metaphor that the Targum renders interpretively to mean "greatest among his sons" just as a firstborn bull is the choicest among the young of the animal. The Pal. Tgs. are more elaborate—Tg. Neof., and the Frg. Tg. (P, V)—"Firstborn rights and kingship as well as glory and grandeur belong to Joseph," and Tg. Ps.-Jon. "the firstborn rights were due to Reuben but were taken from him and given to Joseph from the beginning. . . . "

[46]The Hebrew has: "and his horns are like the horns of a wild ox." It appears from the motifs of this verse, especially the way it was rendered by the Targum, that the main subject here is the Messiah, specifically the Messiah from the House of Joseph, since that particular tribe is mentioned by name. The Targum renders the Hebrew figure of speech, a combination metaphor-simile, by "mighty deeds were done for him by the One who has power and dignity," with "him" referring to the Messiah and "power and dignity" here symbolized by the two horns. The following phrase "by his might (in place of Hebrew 'by them') he kills (in place of the Hebrew 'gores' applicable to the bull) nations instantaneously till the ends of the earth" is a genuine Messianic motif. This approach finds parallels in the following Midrashim:

1. *Ber. Rab.* XLVI:28, p. 213 "'like the bullock' (Isa. 65:25) this (refers to) Messiah ben Joseph who is called 'bull,' as it says: 'a firstborn bull' (Deut. 33:17)."

2. *Shoḥ. Tob* XCII:10, p. 409 ". . . so does the son of David (= the Messiah) attack all four corners of the world, and concerning him Moses said 'Like a firstborn bull in its majesty, his horns are like the horns of a wild ox' (Deut. 33:17)."

The Pal. Tgs. (Neof., Ps.-Jon., and the Frg. Tg. [P, V]) interpret the verse to apply to Joshua's and Gideon's triumphs, being descendants of Ephraim and Manasseh, respectively.

[47]An insertion implied in the Hebrew.

[48]These two changes, expanding the concise and vague Hebrew "in your going out" to refer to waging war against the enemy, and interpreting "in your tents" to mean—when going to celebrate the festival periods in Jerusalem, contrast with the Pal. Tgs. (Frg. Tg. [P, V], Neof. and Ps.-Jon.) all of whom render the first part—"when you go out for trade" and the second "when you are seated in the study halls." As for the first expansion depicting the Zebulunites as going out to war, they are indeed so characterized in 1 Chr. 12:33 "Of Zebulun, such as went forth to battle, expert in war, with all instruments of war, fifty thousand, who could put themselves in array with an undivided heart." The following Midrash elaborates on this theme—Lev.

now these are the myriads of Ephraim
and these are the thousands of
Manasseh."

18. Concerning Zebulun he said,
"Rejoice, O Zebulun, when you go out *to wage war against your enemies,*[48]
and Issakhar *when you go to celebrate the festival periods in Jerusalem.*[48]

19. *The tribes of Israel*[i49] shall assemble at the
Temple Mount;[50]
there they shall slaughter the sacred offerings *for acceptance is there,*[51]
for they will consume the properties of the nations,[52]

Notes, Chapter 33 (Cont.)

Rab. XXV:2 p. 571 "Said R. Tanḥuma: If any one goes out to war and does not concentrate his attention on the battle, he will eventually fall in the battle. The tribe of Zebulun, however, whether they concentrated or not, when they went out to war they were victorious, hence it is written 'Of Zebulun such as went forth to battle . . .' (1 Chr. 12:33)."

The characterization of the Issakharites as celebrating the festival periods in Jerusalem is depicted first and foremost in the following Midrash according to which they were experts in fixing the calendar as a result of their knowledge of the time periods (a fact mentioned in 1 Chr. 12:32) and consequently knew when the festival periods had to be celebrated:

Esth. Rab. IV:1 "'Then the king said to the wise men who knew the times' (Esth. 1:13). Who were these? Rabbi Simon said: This was the tribe of Issakhar, as it says: 'And the Issakharites were men that had understanding of the times to know what Israel ought to do' (1 Chr. 12:32). Rabbi Tanḥuma said: This means for fixing the calendar. Rabbi Jose ben Kazrath said: For intercalation . . . 'The heads of them were 200' (*ibid.*)—these are the 200 presidents of the Sanhedrin which the tribe of Issakhar produced."

The mention of Jerusalem by the Targum here, of course, implies the Temple and the connection of the Issakharites with the Temple is reflected in the Midrash—Ber. Rab. XLIX:14-15, p. 242: "Likewise, Moses said: 'And Issakhar in your tents' (Deut. 33:18), teaching that the Temple was due to have been built in his territory."

[49]The Hebrew has: "people" which the Targum translates as referring to Israel, an interpretation reflected in the following Midrashic texts:

1. *Otiyot de R. Aqiba* (Vers. A, p. 362) ". . . and 'people' means only Israel, as it says: 'they shall call the people to the mountain' (Deut. 33:19)."

2. *Mid. Tan. to Deut.* XXXIII:3, p. 212 "Another explanation for "Indeed He loved the people' (Deut. 33:3) this is Israel, as it says 'they shall call the people to the mountain' (Deut. 33:19)."

Cf. also vs. 3, n. 8 above where a similar identification is made in the Targum.

The Pal. Tgs. differ as to the identification of "people" here; according to Tg. Neof. and the Frg. Tg. (V) the reference is to "the people of the House of Zebulun," while Tg. Ps.-Jon. takes it to refer to "many nations," an identification also reflected in Sifre (*ibid.* CCCLIV, p. 416).

[50]The Hebrew has simply: "mountain" which the Targum, as well as all the Pal. Tgs. (Neof., Ps.-Jon. and the Frg. Tg. [V]) identify as "the mountain of the Holy Temple." The following Midrash—*Otiyot de Rabbi Aqiba* [*ibid.*] is in agreement: "now 'mountain' (Deut. 33:19) means only the Holy Temple, as it says: 'And many peoples shall go and say: Come, let us go up to the mountain of the Lord' (Isa. 2:3)."

[51]An insertion identical to the one made in vs. 10 above, for which see n. 31.

[52]The Hebrew has: "for they will suck of the abundance of the seas" a symbolic characterization which the Targum interprets to refer to Israel's "consumption" (for the figurative "suck") of the "properties," (referred to in the Hebrew by "abundance") of the "nations" (characterized as "seas," the Hebrew *'ammîm* and *yammîm* being used as a play on words). The Sifre (*ibid.*) likewise connects "seas" with "nations" but uses "kingdom" instead.

and the treasures hidden in the sand *will be revealed*
to them."[53]

20. Concerning Gad he said
"Blessed be He who enlarges Gad;
he is poised like a lion
and *kills rulers along with*
kings.[54]

21. *Now he received his own from the start,*[55] for there *in his inherited*
territory,[56]
Moses the great scribe of Israel
is buried;[j57]

Apparatus, Chapter 33 (Cont.)

[j] Ibn Ganaḥ has: "hidden."

[k] G and V have: "the southern area," while Sperber's main text has: "its southern areas."

Notes, Chapter 33 (Cont.)

[53]An addition to complement the verb "consume" of the preceding clause.

[54]The Hebrew "tear" referring to the lion is rendered "kill" in referring to the tribe of Gad which is here likened to a lion in this simile. In the same vein "arm along with scalp" referring to the prey of the lion is rendered "rulers along with kings" in referring to Gad's victims instead.

[55]The Hebrew has: "He saw the best (lit. first) part for himself" and undoubtedly refers back to Num. 32:1 where the observation of the Gadites (together with that of the Reubenites) is described as "Now, the Reubenites and Gadites had a great multitude of cattle, so when they *saw* the land of Jazer and the land of Gilead to be an area (suitable for) cattle . . . " The Targum renders "saw" by "received" referring to the final consummation of their original request for the land of Transjordan. The Hebrew *rē'šît* is translated as an adverb rather than as a noun as if the word read *berē'šît,* hence *beqadmêṯā'.*

[56]The Hebrew has: "the portion of" which is concise and vague. The Targum therefore renders it explicitly by the noun *'aḥsantā',* usually reserved for Hebrew *naḥălāh*—"inheritance" or *'aḥuzzāh*—"possession" and best rendered "inherited possession," and adds the third person singular pronominal suffix for emphasis.

[57]The Hebrew *mĕḥōqēq sāp̄ûn* "an esteemed leader" is understood by the Targum to refer to Moses, with the passive participle *sāp̄ûn* < *spn* as if derived from *ṣpn* "hidden" (t. Sot. IV:8 actually has *ṣap̄ûn* here), thus the translation "buried," an interpretation which existed widely throughout Rabbinic literature, of which a few representative selections follow:

1. *Sifre* [*ibid.* CCCLV, p. 417) "'for there was the portion of an esteemed leader' (Deut. 33:21)—this refers to the burial site of Moses which was placed in Gad's portion."

2. *'Abot R. Nat.* (Vers. BXXV, p. 51) "Now how do we know that he (Moses) was buried in the territory of the Gadites, as it says: 'and to Gad he said: Blessed is He who enlarges Gad, etc. . . . and he saw the best part for himself for there was the portion of an esteemed leader' (Deut. 33:20, 21). "

3. *b. Sot.* 13b ". . . and where was Moses buried? In the territory of Gad, as it is written 'and he saw the best part for himself, etc.' (Deut. 33:21).'

Cf. also y. Sot. 1:10, p. 17c; Mid. Tan. to Deut. XXXIV:5, p. 225; t. Sot IV:8; Ber. Rab. XXXIV:27, p. 170; Sifre *Bĕha'ălōtĕkā* CVI, p. 105; Cant. Zut. 1:17, p. 22.

The Pal. Tgs. render similarly, the Tg. Ps.-Jon. being the most elaborate—"for there, a place paved with precious stones and pearls, in which Moses the scribe of Israel was hidden," while the Frg. Tg. (V and P) as well as Tg. Neof. have "for there Moses the prophet, the scribe of Israel, is buried."

The name *meḥōqēq* rendered "scribe" by the Tg. as well as by all the Pal. Tgs., is a tradition that also exists in the following Rabbinic texts:

1. *b. B. Bat.* 15a ". . . it is written: "Would that they were *inscribed* in a book' (Job 19:23), and it is Moses who is called 'inscriber,' as it is written: 'And he saw the best part for himself,' for there was the portion of an esteemed leader *mĕḥōqēq,* lit. inscriber." Thus *mĕḥōqēq* = scribe.

he went out and went in at[58] the head of the
people;
he performed *righteous deeds*[32]
before[37]
the Lord and his judgments concerning Israel."
22. Concerning Dan he said,
"Dan is *as powerful as*[59] a lion's cub;
his territory is watered by the streams that flow[60] from *Matnan.*"[61]
23. Concerning Naphtali he said,
"Naphtali is sated and abounding with the blessings *from before*[37] the Lord;
he shall inherit the *western area of the Sea of Gennesaret*[62]
and *the southern areas.*"[k]
24. Concerning Asher he said,
"Asher is blessed *with more blessings*[63] than are the <other> sons,
may he be acceptable to his brothers *and be reared on the dainties of*

Notes, Chapter 33 (Cont.)

2. *Otiyot de R. Aqiba* (Vers. A, p. 385) "'By the *mĕḥōqēq*' because all say 'Halakha of Moses from Sinai,' who was called *mĕḥōqēq*, as it is said: "for there was the part of an esteemed leader' (Deut. 33:21). And why was he called *mĕḥōqēq*? Because he inscribed (*ḥqq*) every letter of the Torah with the fingers of his hand."

Cf. also Mid. Tan. to Deut. III:26, p. 18.

[58]The Hebrew has *wayēṯē' rā'šê* which the Targum as well as the Pal. Tgs. (Ps.-Jon., Neof. and the Frg. Tg. [P, V]) understood to refer to Moses' activity as leader of the people idiomatically expressed in Deut. 31:2 and in Num. 27:17 as "going out and coming in." Thus the Targum has *npq* ("going out") and *'ll* ("coming in"), while the Pal. Tgs. have it in reverse order, and the Syr. has "going out" only. The Targum then (as do all the Pal. Tgs. and the Syr.) adds "at" implied in the concise poetic Hebrew.

[59]The Targum converts the Hebrew metaphor into a simile.

[60]An elaborate paraphrase of the Hebrew "leaping forth" which applies to the lion, but translated by the Targum into "his territory is watered by the streams" and applied to them is rendered "that flow."

[61]See Num. Chap. 21, n. 23.

[62]The Hebrew has simply: "the sea," which the Targum renders to specifically refer to the "Western Sea of Gennesaret" as do the Frg. Tg. (V) and Tg. Neof., the latter with a slight emendation; whereas Tg. Ps.-Jon. has the Sea of Sofne and the Sea of Tiberias, the latter also occurring in Sifre (*ibid.*, p. 419): "'Sea' (Deut. 33:23) refers to the Sea of Sofne and 'south' (*ibid.*) refers to the Sea of Tiberias." The Tosefta (t. B. Qam. VIII:18) records the following difference of opinion between R. Jose the Galilean and R. Aqiba: "The tribes did not catch fish from the Sea of Tiberias because it was in the territory of Naphtali . . . as it says: 'possess the sea and the south' (Deut. 33:23), (these are) the words of R. Jose the Galilean. R. Aqiba says: it ('sea') refers to the Sea of Sofne and 'south' refers to the Sea of Tiberias, 'possess' refers to the Great Sea (= Mediterranean)." This debate is also found in the Jerusalem Talmud (y. B. Bat. V:1, p. 15a, although there, only R. Aqiba's opinion is stated in full), as well as in Ber. Rab. XLIX:21, p. 247 with the following important difference—"R. Aqiba says: 'Sea' refers to the Sea of Tiberias and 'South' refers to the Sea of Tiberias." "The Babylonian Talmud (b. B. Qam. 81b) states it anonymously: "Our Rabbis taught: The Sea of Tiberias was included in the portion of Naphtali. In addition he received a rope's length of dry land on the southern side to keep nets on, in fulfillment of the verse: 'possess the sea and the south' (Deut. 33:23)."

This identification of this body with the Sea of Gennesaret comes from the following two Midrashim, according to which 'sea' in this verse refers to the Sea of Kinneret (= Genneserat): PRE XVIII and Shoḥ. Tob. XCII:2, p. 402, the latter of which is hereby cited: "I have created seven seas, and from all of them I only chose the Sea of Kinneret and gave it as an inheritance to the tribe of Naphtali, as it says: 'sated with favor and full of the Lord's blessing; possess the sea and the south!'"

[63]An insertion specifying just how Asher was blessed more than the other sons.

kings.[64]
25. Your *dwelling*[65] should be *as strong as*[66] iron and copper;
your strength {as strong} as the *days of your youth.*[67]
26. There is no god *but*[l] the God of *Israel,*[14] *whose Shekhinah*[68]
in heaven is your support,
and whose *power is in the highest*[m] heavens,
27. the habitation of *God*[n] is since eternity,
by whose Memra[o] *the world was made;*[69]
and He will expel *the*[p] enemy before you
and say: Destroy!
28. Then Israel *will dwell*[q] by *itself*[r] in safety
according to the blessing which their ancestor Jacob pronounced upon them,[70]
in[s] a land producing grain and wine,
even the heavens *that are above them*[71] will *serve them*[72] (with) dew.
29. Happy are you, O Israel, there is no one like you;
a people whose redemption comes *from before*[37] the Lord,
the *strength*[73] of your support,
and from before whom come your powerful triumphs;[74]
your adversaries will deceive you but you will trample on *the joint*[t] *of the necks of their kings."*[75]

Apparatus, Chapter 33 (Cont.)

[l] G, V, and j1 have: "like," as does the Hebrew.
[m] l has: "extends up towards."
[n] n has: "your God."
[o] D, b, and g have: "and by His Memra."
[p] h has: "your."
[q] V, b, *d, and g have: "dwelt," as does the Hebrew.
[r] G has: "themselves."
[s] So also d and s, whereas i, b, and g have: "to," as does the Hebrew. Sperber's main text has: "like," and the Sam. Heb. has: "upon."
[t] b and g have the plural.

Apparatus, Chapter 34

[a] So also Sperber's main text, whereas b, g, and s have: "hinder." Cf. Deut. 11:24.

Notes, Chapter 33 (Cont.)

[64]This addition was, no doubt, influenced by the end of Gen. 49:20 where it exists in the Hebrew.

[65]The Hebrew has the figurative "door/gate bolts" which the Targum renders into its intended meaning.

[66]The Targum converts the Hebrew metaphor into a simile.

[67]The Hebrew has: "your days." The Targum expands the concise and somewhat difficult Hebrew to refer to "the days of your youth," an interpretation that is more clearly expanded in the Pal. Tgs. (Neof. Ps.-Jon. and the Frg. Tg. [P, V]) "and as the days of their youth, so shall be the days of their old age." It is also reflected in Ber. Rab. XLIX:20, p. 268 "'and your strength will equal your days' (Deut. 33:25)—as the days

CHAPTER 34

1. Then from the plains of Moab, Moses ascended Mount Nebo to the summit of the *height*[1] which is opposite Jericho, and the Lord showed him the entire land: Gilead as far as Dan; 2. and all of Naphtali and the territory of Ephraim and Manasseh, as well as all of the territory of Judah as far as the *Western*[a] Sea, 3. and the south and the Plain—the valley of Jericho, the city of palm trees—as far as Zoar. 4. Then the Lord

Notes, Chapter 33 (Cont.)

of your youth so shall be the days of your old age."

The following Midrash is even more specific in details—*Eliyahu Rabba* (IX) X, p. 52 "... and then Asher was told: 'and your strength will equal your days' (Deut. 33:25). Hence it was said [of Asher's daughters that the oldest one of them] looked like a maiden whose menses had not yet begun. [And what God did for the tribe of Asher, He does, and will do, for all the tribes of Israel], as it is said: 'Your strength will equal your days,' i.e., like young shall your elderly be." W.G. Braude and J.J. Kapstein in their annotated English translation of this Midrash (*Tanna Dĕbe Eliyahu: The Lore of the School of Elijah.* Philadelphia [Jewish Publication Society of America], 1981, p. 159, n. 20) point out that by metathesis Hebrew *db'k* ("your strength") may be read *d'bk* ("your sorrow"), hence "your state of being elderly."

[68]The Hebrew "'rider' (of the heavens)" is not an appropriate term applicable to God. Consequently, the Targum translates it with *Shekhinah,* for which see Introduction VII D:3.

[69]The Hebrew: "and underneath are the everlasting arms" is difficult and here interpretively rendered as follows: "the world" remains the object, the predicate "was made" is supplied, and "everlasting arms" is taken to be the indirect object which, referring to God, is consequently rendered into the Memra due to its anthropomorphism.

[70]The Hebrew "Jacob's fountain" is concise and vague. Accordingly, the Targum expands by taking the Hebrew *'ēn* ("fountain") and adding the *k* of comparison prefix which resulted in the Aramaic *kĕ'ēn* "like," then expands it to "the blessing which Jacob their ancestor pronounced on them." This expansion is also contained in the Frg. Tg. (V), Tg. Ps.-Jon., and Tg. Neof., all of whom have *mĕ'ēn*—"in the manner of" instead of *kĕ'ēn* (there exists even one variant in Onq. that has *lĕ'ēn* [l], though with no change of meaning.) The Sifre (*ibid.* CCCLVI, p. 423) reflects this expansion: "'the fountain of Jacob' (Deut. 33:28), with the blessing that Jacob blessed them, as it says: 'may the Lord be with you' (Gen. 48:21)."

[71]The Hebrew has: "his heavens," a figurative way of expressing the heavens that are above Israel. Accordingly the Targum paraphrases "that are above them" in agreement with the phrase "the heavens from above" in Gen. 49:25.

[72]The Hebrew "drip" is figurative and accordingly rendered into its intended meaning.

[73]The Hebrew "shield" a weapon used by humans is here rendered "strength" more applicable to God. See also Gen. 15:1 and n. 2 there. The Pal. Tgs., however, are literal here, Ps.-Jon. using the Aramaic *trîs,* as does the Frg. Tg. (P), while (V) and Tg. Neof. have the Hebrew *mgn.*

[74]The Hebrew "your triumphant sword" is here paraphrased out of respect for God, as it is not deferential for God to be called by this term any more than being called "shield," for which see preceding note.

[75]The Hebrew has: "their backs" or "high places," which the Targum interpretively renders to refer to the joint(s) of the necks of their kings," an interpretation also reflected in the following Sifre (*ibid.* p. 425): "'but you will trample upon their backs/high places' (Deut. 33:29), as it says: (When they had brought all these kings to Joshua), he summoned all the men of Israel and said to the army commanders who had come with him: 'Come here and put your feet on the necks of these kings.' So they came forward and put their feet on their necks." Thus, according to this Midrash, the reference is to a specific incident in history, and the Targum without mentioning Joshua by name is referring to it as well. Tg. Ps.-Jon. and Neof. are identical to Onqelos, while the Frg. Tg. (P) has "on the joints of your enemies" and (V) "on the joints of your kings."

Notes, Chapter 34

[1]See Num. Chap. 21, n. 15.

said to him, "This is the land that I swore to Abraham, (to) Isaac, and (to) Jacob saying: I will give it to your descendants; I have let you see it with your <own> eyes, but you will not cross there." 5. So Moses the servant of the Lord died there in the land of Moab by the *Memra*[2] of the Lord. 6. He buried him in a valley *in the land of Moab*[b] near Beth-Peor, and no one knows his burial place to this day. 7. Now Moses was a hundred and twenty years old when he died; his eye was undimmed *and the radiance of the glory of his face remained unchanged.*[3] 8. Thereupon the Israelites bewailed Moses in the Plains of Moab {for} thirty days, and the wailing period in mourning for Moses came to an end. 9. Now Joshua, son of Nun, *was filled with*[c] the spirit of wisdom, for Moses had laid his hands upon him; and the Israelites *listened to*[4] him and did as the Lord had commanded Moses. 10. Never since then did there ever arise in Israel a prophet like Moses, *to whom the Lord revealed Himself*[5] *face to face,*[6] 11. for all the signs and wonders which the Lord sent him to perform in the land of Egypt, to Pharoah and to all his officials and to his entire land, 12. and for all the mighty power and for all the great *manifestations*[7] that Moses displayed in the sight of all of Israel.

Apparatus, Chapter 34 (Cont.)

[b] j omits.

[c] D has: "was full of," as does the Hebrew.

Notes, Chapter 34 (Cont.)

[2]See Introduction VII D.1.

[3]The Hebrew "and his strength unabated" is here paraphrased by the Targum with reference to the situation described in Exod. 34:30-35 where in vss. 30 and 35 the subject is the increase in the radiance of the glory upon Moses' face. The Targum renders the rare Hebrew *lēḥōh,* "his strength" by that radiance of the glory of Moses' face and the predicate *nās* lit. "flee," by the more applicable "change." CTgF, the Frg. Tg. (V), and Tg. Neof. are somewhat similar, translating "the radiance of his face."

[4]Lit. "accepted from," for which see Gen. Chap. 16, n. 1.

[5]See Gen. Chap. 3, n. 1.

[6]Unlike Exod. 33:11 where the identical Hebrew expression is rendered "word by word" or "literally," here it is rendered in a literal translation of the Hebrew "face to face." The Tgs. Neof., Ps.-Jon., and CTgF, as well as MS Nürnberg in Klein (236), however, render it here identically to the way Tg. Onq. rendered in Exod. 33:11. Onqelos' literal translation may be connected to the following Sifre (*Wĕzōʾt Haḇĕrāḵā* CCLVII, p. 431) according to which this situation holds true only just prior to death: "'Whom the Lord knew face to face' (Deut. 34:10). Why does it say so? Since it says: 'and he said: Show me now Your glory' (Exod. 34:18). He said to him: In this world you shall not see it which is compared to the face, as it says: 'You shall not be able to see My face' (*ibid.,* 20), but you will see it in the world to come which is compared to the back, as it says: 'and I will remove My palm and you will see My back' (*ibid.,* vs. 20). *When did He show it to him? Just prior to death.* This teaches that the dead see (God)."

[7]See Gen. Chap. 21, n. 7.

TAM WELO NISHLAM

Bibliography

BIBLIOGRAPHY

Adler, N., *Netina La-Ger* in Pentateuch Edition *Sefer Torat Elohim.* Wilna, 1886.

Behaq, J., *Tosefot Milu'im.* Warsaw, 1898.

Berkowitz, B.Z.J., *Halifot Semalot.* Wilna, 1874.

Berkowitz, B.Z.J., *Simlat Ger* in *Leḥem Wesimla.* Wilna, 1850-55.

Berkowitz, B.Z.J., *Ote Or* in *Leḥem Wesimla.* Wilna, 1850-55.

Berkowitz, B.Z.J., *Liwyat Ḥen* in *Avne Ziyon.* Wilna, 1877.

Berliner, A., *Einleiting zum Targum Onkelos.* Berlin, 1884.

Braude, W.G. and Kapstein, J.J., *Tanna Debe Eliyahu: The Lore of the School of Elijah.* Philadelphia (Jewish Publication Society of America), 1981.

Churgin, P., "The Halakha in Targum Onqelos" (in Hebrew) *Talpiyot* 2 (1945-46).

Driver, S.R., *Deuteronomy: A Critical and Exegetical Commentary.* International Critical Commentary. New York, 1902.

Grossfeld, B., "Neofiti 1 to Deut 31:7—The Problem re-Analyzed." *ABR* 24 (1976):30-34.

Grossfeld, B., "Targum Neofiti to Deut 31:7." *JBL* 91 (1972):533-534.

Hoffmann, D., ed., *Midrash Tannaim to Deuteronomy.* Berlin, 1909.

Korah, Y., *Marpe Lashon in Sefer Keter Tora: Ha-Ta'ağ Hagadol.* Jerusalem, 1960.

Löwenstein, M., *Nefesh Ha-Ger.* Deuteronomy. Pietrokov, 1912.

Markon, Z., *Mi-Sifrotenu Ha-Atiqa.* Wilna, 1910.

Melamed, E.Z., *The Onomastikon of Eusebius.* Jerusalem, (The Hebrew University), 1966.

Payne-Smith, J., ed., *A Compendious Syriac Dictionary.* Oxford (At the Clarendon Press), 1957.

Pellett, D.C., "Trachonitis" in *Interpreter's Dictionary of the Bible* 4 (1962):676-677.

Rosenbaum, M. and Silbermann, A.M., *Pentateuch with Targum Onkelos, Haphtaroth and Rashi's Commentary.* New York (Hebrew Publishing Company), 1934.

Rosenthal, F., *Beth Talmud* 2 (1882): 274-285.

Schefftel, B., *Bi'ure Onqelos.* Munich, 1888.

Sperber, A., *The Bible in Aramaic Vol.* III. *The Latter Prophets. According to Targum Jonathan.* Leiden, (E.J. Brill), 1962.

Vermes, G., "Lebanon" in *Scripture and Tradition in Judaism: Haggadic Studies. Studia* Post-Biblica IV. Leiden (E.J. Brill), 1961.

Vermes, G., "'Car le Liban, c'est le consil de la communaute.' note sur Pésher d'Habacuc, 12, 3-4." *Melanges biblique, Paris, 1957.*

Wertheimer, A.J., ed., *Batei Midrashot.* Second edition. Jerusalem (Ktab Wasepher), 1968.

Wertheimer, S.A., *Or Ha-Targum.* Jerusalem, 1935.

Indexes

BIBLICAL

TARGUMIM

Targum Onkelos

Pseudo-Jonathan

Neofiti I

Neofiti M

Neofiti M_1

Neofiti M_2

Fragment Targum

CTgD

Targum Nebi'im

Targum Ketubim

CTgF

RABBINIC

I. TOSEFTA, MISHNA, TALMUD

II. MIDRASH

POST-BIBLICAL

New Testament

Historians

Church Fathers

Ancient Versions

Samaritan Hebrew

Samaritan Targum

Septuagint

Commentaries

AUTHORS